Reflections On Life II

Notes from the Journey

Copyright © Staci Stallings, 2007

Published by:
Spirit Light Publishing
Amarillo, TX,
through lulu.com
www.lulu.com/spirit-light

Printed in the United States of America

Cover Design, KDJ Outsourcing
design@kdjoutsourcing.com

Library of Congress Cataloging-in-Publication Data
is available upon request.

ISBN
978-0-6151-6099-3

Reflections On Life II

Notes from the Journey

Staci Stallings

*To my readers who have shown me
so much encouragement and love.
May you be blessed and rewarded
as you have blessed and rewarded me
by your kind comments, prayers, and support.*

Reflections On Life II
Notes from the Journey

Lessons as We've Walked in the Garden

On Family

On Being

On Living

On Writing

On God as Life

Give me Your lantern and compass,
give me a map,
So I can find my way to the sacred mountain,
to the place of Your presence,
To enter the place of worship,
meet my exuberant God,
Sing my thanks with a harp,
magnificent God, my God.

(Psalms 43 3-4 TMB)

Foreword

One day not so long ago, a 60-year old retired attorney living in Iowa, who was raised in a Presbyterian Church, received an email from a total stranger who read something he posted on a Christian writer's Internet bulletin board. He had received a lot of similar emails, but for some reason he responded to this one, and the stranger turned out to be a woman slightly more than half his age, living in Texas, who was raised in the Catholic Church. You know what? The Holy Spirit didn't care about any of that; in fact, the Spirit used those differences to Its advantage. Truth is, nothing happens by coincidence when the Holy Spirit is involved.

In the blink of an eye, they became friends, prayed together, wrote together and learned that in Christ there truly is no east nor west, north or south, but only one great fellowship in Him. And the two have never even met face to face, only through the Holy Spirit and its tool, the Internet.

I am that man, and Staci Stallings is that woman. I have been privileged to read several of her works in the last few months including this one, and I challenge anyone to find a better devotional or inspirational source to carry them through the day. The Holy Spirit is truly at work in Staci's writing. Even an older Presbyterian from Iowa can see it, feel it, and be humbled by it. I praise God for Staci's profound insights and intense faith shown clearly and without apology in this book and all her writings. Her writing makes me smile, moves me to tears, drives me to my knees, and forces me to raise my hands in praise, frequently all at the same time. She challenges all readers to dig deeper and expect more from a Godly life. Using everyday examples and observations from her own life, this wife and mother of three, challenges everyone to let God have control, surrender self, and wait patiently for the Holy Spirit to do its work through them.

I humbly invite you to join my friend, Staci, on her journey. No doubt, you'll feel better for the experience.

— Dennis L. Bates, Christian Author

1

Lessons from My Walk
in the Garden

Now the Tree of Life was in the middle of the garden...
(Genesis 2:9)

Your Ultimate GPS

I'm sure by now you've heard of those GPS—Global Positioning Systems—that come in some cars today. This system, with the help of a satellite, can tell you turn by turn how to get wherever you want to go—whether you've ever been in a particular city or not.

It is a map, but it's so much more than that. For one, you don't have to locate your starting destination on the map. The GPS already knows where you are. You don't have to know exactly what you're looking for. If you ask for restaurants, it will give you a list. You may have no idea what section of the city your destination is, but you don't have to know. The GPS does.

Now wouldn't it be cool to have a GPS for your spiritual life too? Think about it. "I want peace." Bing. Here's peace, and here's how to get there. "I want joy." Bing. Turn left at the stoplight.

The truth is we do have a GPS for our spiritual lives. Only it's not a Global Positioning System, it's a God Positioning System.

We all have it. It was installed on our model before we left the factory. Unfortunately many of us don't realize that it wasn't optional, that it's on every model made—even ours. We also don't realize how reliable it is. It's as if we are determined to use the lousy, antiquated maps we've had all our lives rather than have to learn to use something different.

Well, let me tell you, this feature is worth the trouble to learn to use!

The first step is to recognize you *are* equipped with this feature. Recognizing that it's even available is a good first start.

A friend of mine was recently taking a major test that would determine if she could stay in the job she already had. She had failed the first time by one point, so on the morning of the test, she called my sister (a mutual friend) to ask for prayers. My sister said, "If you get stuck, just breathe, and ask that God show you the answer." To which my friend replied, "But isn't that cheating?"

It would be if we were somehow gaining access to some outside source of information, but what we're doing when we do that is gaining access to a source deep inside of us. It's called the Holy Spirit. It is a deep, deep knowing when something is right for us and when something is just not. It is in fact our own personal GPS.

Miraculously, our friend "found" her missing point and passed the test. But the truth is we all have that knowing built into us. The more you use it, the more you will wonder how you ever got along without it. It will become second nature to first ask it for its assistance, and then to count on it as your primary source of guidance.

Using it is not hard. It's a matter of breathing deeply, going deep, and accessing it. I find I use my GPS most often in my writing. I don't "know" the plot point-by-point, but when I surrender to the part of me that does, miracles start showing up in books. Connections I hadn't seen suddenly appear. Turns that I thought made no sense for a character to make suddenly tie the whole story together.

On an earthly plain, I cannot explain this. But on a spiritual plain, I can tell you it happens all the time.

You, too, have a GPS. The question is, are you using it to its fullest capabilities?   (2006)

Which Jonah Are You?

"Sometimes it would be nice to just move to a desert and pray all the time. You know, just be alone with God." That's how my sister described being a stay-at-home mom who keeps others' kids at her home. Now, I only have a three-year-old at home with two others in school, but I completely understood. For those who don't spend days at a time home alone with kids, there is a serious patience-factor present every single minute.

This one wants that. That one wants this. This one's hungry. That one doesn't want whatever you just spent an hour fixing for lunch. Everybody's tired, but nobody wants to take a nap. And then, you get the situation my sister found herself in with random kids getting sick without warning. It's not fun.

Being a woman of God who carries on a near-constant two-way conversation with God as often as not, she looked around her house one day completely exhausted and ready to give up. She hadn't had time to read her Bible or to do anything else for that matter in days. The house was a mess. The kids were screaming. She hadn't had time to sit down and play the piano—one of her favorite spending time with God activities in what seemed like forever. She hadn't even had much time to share her burdens with my mom or me on the phone. So, she was drowning and wishing, as we all do at times, that God had chosen to put her somewhere else in life that wasn't so hectic and demanding.

Then she went to church.

Funny, how when you have turned your "God walkie talkie" on and tuned it to His channel, you will get the answers you most need even when you don't expect it. At church, the readings were about Jonah, and it happened to be at the uplifting part of the story, when Jonah was actually doing what God told him to do—saving

Ninevah.

At the conclusion of the readings, the priest got up to give the sermon, and he said, "Which Jonah are you?" Of course, my sister knew the story of Jonah, but she'd never heard it quite like this.

Now in the Bible story of Jonah, there are several parts that parallel our own experience. There is the call from God to go do something for Him. There is our reluctance to go for whatever reason the ego can come up with. Face it, we're not always Mary saying, "Do unto me according to Your will." There is the futile attempt to run from God. (He can find you, by the way, so running isn't exactly logical.) There is the uplifting part when we actually do what He says to do. And then, there is the part when we get mad that we helped someone we're not sure deserves it and life gets better for them.

If you're honest, I'm sure you relate to at least a couple of these parts of the story. So, the priest asked, "Which Jonah are you?" Are you the Jonah who tries to ignore God's call? Are you the Jonah who tries to run from God's call? Are you the Jonah who snivels and throws a fit over what you are called to do? Or are you the Jonah who does what God's called you to do whether or not you like it or are particularly thrilled with doing it?

My sister said, "Now, how much clearer could that message have been? God called me to be with these kids. He called me to be a wife and a mother. I have no doubt about that, but here I am wanting what He called someone else to do. Up until that moment, I was Jonah sniveling and whining about what God wants me to do." As usual, when you get a lesson, two things happened.

One, she began to appreciate her role in this world in a whole new light; and two, others began to come to her aid to give her a break. In short, she got what she ultimately wanted and needed, but she got the lesson too.

So, I ask you: "Which Jonah are you?"   (2006)

When Evil Turns

Have you ever noticed how beautiful evil is the first time you encounter it? It looks fun and exciting, like the answer to all of your problems. Whether it's that first drink, that large bag of chips, that joint—or even those less obvious introductions—like that first time a little lie will remedy a situation and "no one will ever know," or that first time tired seems more important than church, or that first time you realize your friends all curse and you join in to feel a part of something. Boy, do you feel big. It's as if for the first time in your life, you finally fit in. Yes, this finally is the answer you've been looking for.

If and when you take that first step toward evil, the next is much easier, and the next easier than that. Evil looks at you softly, knowing it has you already, but wanting only to lead you further, deeper into the darkness. It doesn't show you the darkness to which you are heading, instead it holds out false light, false beliefs, false hope. It will convince you one experience at a time that yes, indeed you have finally found "the answer." It will convince you that this, finally, will take away all the bad things in your life. It will help you to escape from feeling separated, alone, and scared. It will make you feel like somebody.

Oh, yes. Evil looks beautiful—at first.

I've always sensed this fact. I've always kind of known that evil doesn't look evil the first time we encounter it, the first time it tempts us toward its side. However, that understanding was never put into so concrete terms until I saw *The Chronicles of Narnia: The Lion, The Witch, and The Wardrobe*. In the movie, as in the book, the character of Edmund stumbles into the realm of the Witch, who is evil personified perfectly. She is not a hideous, deformed creature. No, she is beautiful in an icy, sinister way.

At their first meeting, the Witch instantly sizes Edmund up as the way she can get what she wants—a way to kill those who are meant to destroy her. But rather than demand anything from Edmund, instead she "sweetens him up" literally. She feeds him beautiful, delicious Turkish Delights. And while she feeds his body empty magic, she feeds his mind empty magic as well. If he will just be on her side, if he will bring his brother and sisters to her, she will not only give him more Turkish Delight, she will make him a king with his brother as his servant.

This, of course, sounds as wonderful to Edmund as it does to us. You see for me, the Turkish Delight was success, achievement, and accomplishment; and being a queen meant my work would be recognized and revered. Now, the insidious thing about this for me is that Satan used something that looked holy and good to lead me further onto his side. I was using my writing to serve God. I was working for God. I wanted to be published so I could spread God's word to all the world. Such a noble goal that, and so ultimately hollow and untrue because my efforts were just that *mine* not His.

"I will give you all of this…" That's what Satan told Christ as they stood on the mountaintop, and that's always where Evil starts with us. He doesn't start at the throw us down on a cross and crucify us part although whether we turn to his side or not, that is always, *always* where we end up when the world is in charge of things.

You see, Satan doesn't care about us except for how we can help him further himself. (And it is the same with evil people in the world as well.) As soon as we are no longer needed to further his goals and ambitions, we are expendable. Worse, when we realize he thinks so little of us and we try to turn from him, our death and destruction inevitably results from his innate, seething anger and his distrust of us. In fact, he knows better than we do where evil leads—into a selfish, jealous, power-hungry pit of separation, desperation, and fear, and if we continue to follow it, we might even become more evil than he is, and he can't have us be the ruler of *his* domain. So, our destruction at his hand is inevitable at the outset of his plan. All he really cares about is using us until we are no longer needed to further his purposes.

In the movie, Edmund is taken in by the Witch's treats so much so that he voluntarily leaves his brother and sisters to seek her out. He crosses a great wood and a mountain range to get to her because he believes her to be his only friend. Let me tell you, when Satan convinces you that he is your only friend, you're in serious trouble. Upon entering the Witch-queen's palace which is a cold, lifeless place, Edmund is at first afraid. Then he realizes how "superior" he is to those who are now stone statues in the Witch's "kingdom."

It is telling how very few lives there are in her kingdom. Only the three servants who do her bidding are animated with life. That should've been a hint to get out of there, but of course, we always think that we are the favored one of her majesty, Evil. These others were just dumb about it. This could never happen to us. And so we are drawn deeper and deeper into the lies she has us believing are real.

After a heart-stopping moment with the queen's guard, Edmund is led into the queen's throne room, and for one more moment he is allowed to believe the illusion. Symbolically, he walks up to her throne and sits on it. He has done exactly what got Satan tossed from Heaven. He has pictured himself on that throne and wanted it for himself—not for the benefit of anyone else but because it shows his power and his right to be lord over everyone else.

Immediately, however, we see the Witch, the queen herself standing, watching him. She sees Edmund, sitting on her throne, and in that moment, the turn happens. You can see it in her eyes and her countenance as her eyes narrow and her face drops to a malicious scowl. Then, for one more moment, she pulls the illusion of nice back to her as she steps over to him. "Like it?" she asks.

And that is exactly what Satan asks us. "Like it?" Then he smiles because he knows we have truly fallen for the ultimate lie.

Edmund, knowing he has overstepped his place, jumps out of the chair, but it's too late for him. She has him, and she knows it even if he doesn't. The next scene is telling. She questions him about his service for her, and he tries to talk his way out of why he hasn't done what she told him to do. Then, humanly although stupidly, he asks for more Turkish Delight.

The next that we see Edmund, he is literally in shackles and chains. Very poignant symbolism because when we have begun to see evil for what it truly is, we are instantly chained to keep us enslaved to its bidding. To us, these "chains" may look like a lot of things—habits that we can't break, addictions that have a hold on us, friends we don't want to turn our backs on because they've been nice to us in the past, ways of living that are so comfortable that we don't want to risk doing it a different way, guilt for all the things we should have done differently, a need for money just to survive, and the ultimate chain, not seeing that life could ever be any better than it is at that horrific moment.

Edmund is now given not Turkish Delights but stale bread and air for water. He's miserable. He knows he made a huge mistake, but how to get out of it? The saddest component of this part of the tale is how intensely he's trying to do the right thing but how acutely clear it is that HE has to do the right thing. There is no back up. There is no guide. There is no one to help him. Just him and his own resources fighting to do the right thing in the coldest, scariest place in the world.

For me, this moment was when I realized how empty the world's acclaim ultimately was. I had spent two solid weeks traveling to do book signings and appearances only to come home depleted and empty. Whatever book sales were needed to make me feel "successful" hadn't been met (and no matter how many you sell, you could always have sold more).

Then my publicist emailed telling me she was going to get a copy of the television appearance with the intention of judging my performance. I now see this as the way the world does everything. You have to know what you're doing (even if you don't), and then what you did is picked apart—supposedly to make you better, but we all know the lie that really is. Being picked apart may seem like it works because we've seen people who are pushed to their limits and beyond, who are going on their own power to get better, and it looks like that works. However, I submit to you that the "acclaim" the world holds out as your reward will feel like smoke in your hands if that is all you end up with. And it's not hard to see that if that's all you're going for, that's all you will end up with—even if you get it. Emptiness will be all you have to hold onto because that's the way Satan has set it up.

It is at this point in the movie that Edmund is again and again made to look at what he's done to those around him. The faun that Edmund so innocently turned in is brought before him and told of Edmund's betrayal. Edmund's guilt crashes in on him. Then the Witch uses the faun, beating him as Edmund watches to get Edmund's cooperation. By this point, Satan is willing to beat anyone, knowing that on our own we will feel so helpless that we will do whatever he asks just to get it to stop.

And then he smiles at our helpless weakness. In minutes Edmund sees that even though he gave the Witch what she wanted to get her to stop beating the faun, ultimately she turned the faun to stone anyway. I think at that point Edmund is beginning to see that this will not end well for him. Going on your own devises, there is no way out once you've sold your soul to evil.

Thus begins a trek through the wood—deeper and darker the world becomes, and when we see Edmund again, he is bound to a tree, defenseless against the jabs and jibes of all the evil around him. He's been beaten, and by now, he knows full-well that he took the wrong path, but still he sees no way out.

Of course the story doesn't end there although in our own lives we often think that it does. No, Aslan, the Christ figure, sends a regiment out to rescue Edmund and bring him back into the fold. In a scene that we watch but never hear, Aslan talks with Edmund who is then released of his guilt in the matter fully.

Aslan tells Edmund's brother and two sisters, "What's past is past. You are not to speak of this to Edmund anymore." There is more to the story that you really should see the movie to understand—Edmund being further used by the Witch, her cruelty and utter contempt for Edmund's soul, her cold need to destroy him, how his soul is eventually ransomed and saved by the only one who can. But that is for another lesson.

For now... After the movie, my friend and I were discussing the meaning of this part, and I asked her, "So, when did evil turn on you?" I asked because this insight of evil being so nice to us and leading us to believe that it will be what saves us until we find out the truth was so clear to me.

Without hardly pause to think, she told me the answer for her. Until the moment evil turned, she had twisted her life to be able to gain her family's love. She had made foolish choices for herself in a vain attempt to get their acceptance. Over and over she had let herself down, pushed herself into a corner, and cowed to whatever guilt trip needed to be taken so that they would notice her and love her. What an insidious way for Satan to work because on the outside, her chains looked so loving and helpful and compassionate. Yet they really were chains.

The moment she described (and like Aslan with Edmund I shall let you see the lesson without hearing the actual words) made her see that killing herself and her spirit to gain their love would never work. Whatever she did, it would never be enough, and thinking that it would was a lie.

The journey back for her has been rocky at times, as it is with all of us. She is on the path, and now she sees evil for what it really is, and trusting God's love for her and His path for her is getting if not easier, than clearly easier than the alternative. She is a soul who has seen evil for what it will do to you if you believe it and follow it.

As for me, it was less a single moment than a whole string of them that showed me how empty achievement and success by the world's standards are. The glitz and the gold the world holds out are nothing more than a shiny way to get you to walk toward them. When you get them, they are at first smoke and in the end chains that will destroy you if you don't find a way to grab on to the One who is real.

He is what you need. And He is all you need. Once you get that, really get that, then trying to prove yourself and your worth to anyone else is simply pointless. You have seen evil for what it is, and you no longer need follow its beckoning.

How lucky are you if you are not chained by material things. How lucky are you if you are not addicted to the approval of others. How lucky are you if you do not fall for the delights that the world holds out to you. Yes, how very lucky are you… How lucky are you if you have seen evil turn on you and have used that moment as the incentive to grab onto the only Real Savior of your soul. How lucky are you… How very lucky are you. (2006)

What Everyone Else Says

Talk about confused, my friend was. She kept saying, "I'd just cry and say, 'Lord, please tell me what's the truth.'" Understanding her plight wasn't difficult. She was learning something new and needing for it to be right the first time. So she did what any sane person would do, she asked for help. Only the "help" sounded like this:

"You have to have a lot of details."

"You use too many details."

"I like this section."

(Same section) "This section needs a lot of work."

"I like this character."

(Same character) "I hate this character."

"You need a hook."

"Hooks are for the book, not the cover letter."

"You have to do this." "Don't ever do this."

In short, she was drowning in the sea of conflicting advice.

As we talked, she began to see the conflicting advice for what it was – other people's opinions. As my mom always said, "Give me your opinion. I want to hear it, but I don't have to take it."

My friend was heading the opinions and trying to use all of them, and it was paralyzing her. It's a trap many of us fall into. Everyone has an opinion about how we should be living our lives. We should do this. We have to do this. We can't do that. And many times we get completely conflicting advice. We, too, can be drowning and wondering if there even is a "truth."

After about 15 minutes of hearing about how she didn't understand because all of these advice-givers were multi-published authors, and they should know the truth, in frustration I finally said, "Yes, but they are not God." That stopped her cold.

The truth is that there is no problem with asking for advice, but then you must make the decision for yourself. Some will agree with you. Some will not. But trying to please everybody will soon convince you that nothing you do is right. It will paralyze you, and that's exactly what Satan would love to do.

I suggested that she get quiet, breathe, and listen to what her heart was telling her to do. In all likelihood it won't look like what the world says is "the only thing that will work" because God doesn't work the way the world does. In fact, His direction may sound absolutely crazy (Christ on the cross comes to mind). However, if you don't have Him guiding you, finding "the truth" is all-but impossible.

Five minutes after I got off the phone from our conversation, I got in my van to get my kids from school. Sean Hannity happened to be on the radio talking to a soldier who had been ridiculed by an anti-war protester.

Hannity said, (I paraphrase), "You can't live your life based on what everyone else things – especially if you are to take a real stand. If you make everyone else happy, you will be paralyzed because whatever you do will always be wrong. You have to figure out where you are and be there." After at least a three-minute speech, he took a breath and said, "Whew, I don't know where that came from. Why did I go into that?"

I laughed. It was a message to me verifying what I had just said sent from the Holy Spirit through Sean Hannity over the airwaves even though Sean had no idea that's why he said it. It's pretty cool how the Holy Spirit can get that stuff to work out. (2005)

Two Questions That Change Everything

When you're living with the Holy Spirit, there are many moments when things aren't going the way you thought they would. That's hard. I know. Because when you put everything in His hands, things are supposed to work out the way you wanted them to, right? I understand. Really I do. What I challenge you to see, however, is that sometimes God knows what we want is not really the best of what can be, sometimes we need the lessons only not getting what we want can teach us. He sees that, and He has heard you say you're putting it in His hands and that you trust Him, so He believes you will be patient enough to wait for His perfect timing, His perfect way.

But the truth is, sometimes it just doesn't feel that way. Sometimes His timing drives you completely crazy. Sometimes it is nearly impossible to believe that it will ever happen. Sometimes you just want verification that *something* is happening because it looks like nothing is happening.

A friend of mine was in exactly this dilemma the day we talked. She had made the leap, had sent in the manuscript to the big publisher, and had even gotten back a reply that wasn't an outright rejection, which in the publishing world is cause for serious celebration. Then the requisitions editor added a little phrase that for two months had grated across her patience. "I will get back to you as soon as possible."

She said, "How long is 'as soon as possible' anyway? I thought that would be like a couple weeks tops. Now it's been two months, and still I haven't heard anything. I'm thinking maybe I should write him and tell him to either publish it or reject it, so at least it's settled and I can go on with my life."

I understood her frustration because when you're living in the world, on your own, seeing things from only your perspective, and believing it's all up to you, frustration will naturally occur. Why? Because no matter how right things are now, they could always be better. Yes, you got the manuscript finished. Yes, it was the best you've ever done. Yes, you didn't get the form letter rejection that most often get sent to aspiring writers.

In fact, he liked it. In fact, he said he may ask for more. In fact, this is exactly what you've been praying for since you first typed in that very first word, and yet… Now what?

It's important at moments like this to keep two questions in mind. These two questions in the midst of "This is driving me crazy!" will go a long way to settle your spirit and help you to see what's really going on. They won't give you more patience, but somehow they make patience less necessary.

The first question is this:

Where is my focus?

As life has wrapped around you in a menagerie of directions, have you let your focus fall back into worldly pursuits? In short, is your focus on you or on God? Ah, great question. If your focus is on you, nerves, anger, and impatience are readily evident. You begin to ask questions like, "What should I do?" "How long should I wait?" "What am I doing this for?" And you begin to doubt yourself and your dream. "Maybe this isn't even worth it." "Maybe I should never have even tried." "Maybe I'd be better off trying something else."

When your focus is on you, life is hard. Really hard. No matter what you do, it's never as much as you should have done. No matter where you are, you should be over there. No matter what, life could always be better, and you have a sneaking suspicion that if you could just figure out what everyone else knows, it would be.

On the other hand, when your focus is on God, you trust that you are where you are supposed to be, that things are happening that you can't see that will make the entire enterprise turn out far more wonderfully than you could ever have imagined, and that when it's time to move, He'll let you know. So, where is your focus?

The second question is this:

What is God trying to teach me through this experience?

This is a nice question mostly because it distracts your mind and gives it something to do other than cataloging how awful this is and dragging your focus back to you. However, it's also a very helpful question for a lot of other reasons. The most important being because every situation can teach you something if you are open to the lesson and if you are looking for it. Many people get so caught up in getting to the goal they've set that they close themselves off to other ways success might actually be happening.

For example in my writing, I wanted to sell a lot of books so money would not be a problem My efforts went to making this happen. My time was devoured by it. It consumed me. Then one day I stopped my headlong pursuit of "success" long enough to ask what God was trying to show me through the waiting. Immediately I saw two things. One, the money was not a problem. It just wasn't coming from me but from my husband's booming business. Solve one. Secondly I began to see what I had learned in the waiting.

One of the biggest lessons was getting a really long, hard look at the life of an author with the success I thought I wanted. Jetting off every weekend to book signings or speaking engagements, attending conferences and book fairs. I'm not saying those things are wrong for everyone. But they are wrong for me.

Another was bending who you are in order to get a publishing company to like what you wrote enough for them to publish you. Now many readers don't realize how completely a manuscript can be changed from inception to completion to publication. In fact, my first novel *The Long Way Home* was published with the help of an editor. I will be forever grateful for the things he taught me, but one of those lessons was how little control the author has over what finally goes out.

My editor, for whatever reason, was colon crazy. He would put colons into the manuscript for no apparent reason. He just liked them. After awhile he admitted that some he had put in just to see if I would catch them. I did, but what I didn't catch was how thoroughly he had stripped my voice out of the manuscript. By the time it was finished, it sounded just like every other book on the market. Some call this making a book "marketable," but I'm not so sure. The more I look at what this process does, the more I am convinced the one thing it does with precision is to eradicate the unique voice God gave to the author.

Of course it's always done under the guise of making the work "better" and "marketable" by the world's standards. To which I have to ask, "Where is God in this?"

So, for me, I'm glad God didn't give me the world's definition of success with my novels that I thought I wanted. I would no doubt have run myself and my family into the ground over it. That's one of the things He taught me, and one of the lessons I know I would have missed had not learned to ask the two questions that change everything. (2005)

Thy Will Be Done My Way

A good friend of mine was having a meltdown. The problem was she wanted a fellow traveler on life's journey to have the fabulous spiritual experience she'd had on retreat. Unfortunately she'd become convinced that her presence on the retreat team was making that impossible. Duty said she couldn't leave, but her heart said if she stayed, her friend would be so concerned about her being there that she wouldn't open up, that she would stay in fear and isolation, that her life changing experience would be forever ruined.

There was no doubt that my friend cared. Her caring was immensely evident. In fact, when I was informed of the dilemma as one of the retreat services began, she had already secluded herself from the group because she "just knew" she should leave. The tears were flowing. The regret and the guilt were overrunning the banks of her heart and her lashes. First I gave her a hug because I really hate it when Satan uses our best intentions to take a successful whack at our hearts. There are very few things that make me angrier to be honest. She needed a hug, so that was first.

Then gently I explained how Satan was using her best intentions against her, that what she wanted to happen—her friend to have the best retreat possible—was a noble goal. Unfortunately she had been conned into believing that *she* was who would determine whether or not this would happen. It was heart breaking to watch because she wanted so badly to do what was right, but what was right seemed to lead only to something wrong no matter which way she went.

It became clear as we whisper/talked that the trust she professed to have in God didn't make it all the way to what happens when He puts you in a place that isn't what you expected. I told her it was very possible that her friend needed her to be there, that she needed her presence in order to break through a barrier she wouldn't otherwise have had to face. It was also possible God had set up this very scenario in order to break my friend of the belief that everyone else's happiness, peace, and joy somehow hinged on something she did or didn't do. That seemed a new revelation. Her presence could be helpful—even if it didn't seem that way? Interesting. She might be learning something through this too? What a concept.

I looked at her and said, "It's like you're saying, 'Thy will be done, but it better be done my way.'" She laughed and through the tears she said, "And that's a problem?"

Of course I got the joke. I got it because I've been there.

I first remember this lesson coming to me when the desire to publish first lit into my heart. I had by that time become an expert at putting the writing of the books into God's hands. Over and over again He had shown me to trust in His timing, in His way, in His love as I wrote. Pieces would fall into place that I hadn't seen, couldn't have known prior to the moment I most needed them. Words would just come to me, whole scenes. Whole books that made sense in a way that I couldn't have planned to save my life flowed from my fingertips. The more I trusted, the better they got.

And then I published, trusting that He would make it the success it was destined to be. However, it quickly became clear that what I thought success would look like wasn't what He had in mind at all. I struggled against this, threw money at it, threw effort at it— all to no avail. Success didn't come any faster nor in any greater degree than it ever had.

In the writing I trusted Him, but when it came to marketing and promotion, it just wasn't progressing the way I thought it would. I often prayed, "Thy will be done…" But it was as if there were limits to what I wanted His will to be in charge of, and let me tell you, His will needed to look exactly like what I thought it would, otherwise that just wasn't good enough.

I don't remember the exact moment when it first occurred to me how ridiculous I was being. I just know I now can't believe how blind I was. I mean come on! Talk about "Thy will be done, but it better be done my way."

Thankfully I have learned to put both the process AND the results into His very capable hands. I've learned to see that His definition of success might at first seem very different than mine, but if I trust long enough, I eventually see that what He had in mind is infinitely better than what I had in mind. In fact, it's become abundantly clear to me how miserable I would have been had my will won out.

When you pray that line in the Our Father... "Thy will be done on earth as it is in Heaven" make sure you're not adding a silent "but it better be done my way" with how you're living your life. I guarantee if you are, no matter which "right road" you decide to travel, it will always turn out to be the wrong one. Thy will be done. Period. Plans, process, results, all of it. Forever.

That's success. (2005)

"They"

This was supposed to be a reply to rule mongers in a writing group, but since I don't think "they" will get it anyway, I decided to turn the specific lesson into a general one for any time I come face-to-face with "they." I will tell you from experience that "they" will do everything in their power to assert their power over yours.

They will tell you that whatever you are doing can't be done if you aren't doing it their way. They will shoot you down with words. They will make you believe that they wield the power to keep you from reaching your dream if you don't listen to them and their rules.

This pattern started in the Garden of Eden. There were two trees—the Tree of Life, that was the one where by eating from it, you simply rested in God and let Him take care of everything; and the Tree of the Knowledge of Good and Evil, that was the tree of rules, the one whereby you said, "I can do it on my own just show me what I have to do."

Throughout the Bible over and over again this story is recounted in different ways. Israel is enslaved by Egypt. God tells Moses, "Do what I say, and I will get you out of there." Do what I say to do—not rules but follow the steps I tell you to take. And He opens the Red Sea and He sends manna from Heaven to feed them.

Then as if on cue, the people get restless with God helping them because they don't see where this is leading. So they demand that Moses ask God for a way for them to do it themselves. The result is the Ten Commandments. By the time Moses comes down that mountain, they are already "doing it themselves." They've made a golden calf and are worshiping it. They have replaced God with something they could make on their own.

You would think we would learn, but then several hundred years later when Jesus arrives on the scene, here we are again with the Pharisees. They know all the rules. In fact, they have like 700 rules that people must follow if they want to come worship at the Temple. They are "ruling" people to death. An example is the adulteress. She broke a rule, so now she must be stoned.

Then Jesus shows up. He writes in the sand. He tells the rule mongers, "If you've never broken a rule, then you can cast a stone at her." No one does. Jesus doesn't come at this woman with rules, He handles her with love and compassion and forgiveness.

But still the rule mongers don't get it. They think the rules will make them better. They use the rules to bash and batter others in the name of "helping them." They are just like Eve handing that apple to Adam. "Here, this will help. If you eat it, you will know as much as I do, then you will be able to get your own dream without worrying about God's plan and what He wants for you."

I will tell you this, however, from my research, "they" don't know much. Over and over with people who have really made it— especially in the creative realm—you will hear: "They said I had to do it their way, but that wasn't me so I did it the way my heart said to, and it worked out." Those who really break out tune out "they" and listen instead to their heart, to God whispering softly inside them.

By following God these brave souls defy the common logic. They choose to take sustenance from God rather than eating from the Tree of the Knowledge of Good and Evil (the rules, the you have to's and the you can'ts). They've stopped listening to the "theys" of the world.

It's that example I want to follow. Because like Paul, I've found—God's way works. Trying to follow a bunch of rules that "they" came up with, doesn't. (2006)

The Wrath of God

Growing up I had one of two reactions to the thought of the wrath of God—either that it totally contradicted the image of the God of love or it caused me to utterly fear God's punishment for my transgressions and therefore to fear ever meeting Him in the first place. Which reaction was more prevalent in my spirit, I can't say because when I look, they are pretty much equal. This dichotomy of what the wrath of God means logically threw my understanding of God into swirls of chaos. Which was it?

Did God love me beyond all telling, or was He sitting there with a giant computer going, "Great. She really messed up this time. Add another two days to her fire time"? Obviously the two could not coexist. God could not be all-loving and yet have this terrible desire to throw every sinner into the fire for eternity. Either one or the other, but it couldn't be both.

It wasn't until this weekend that the real meaning of the wrath of God came into focus for me. As usual, the Holy Spirit intersected two seemingly disparate pieces of input into my existence, got me to thinking about them, and then sat back and watched for my epiphany to occur.

The first piece of information came in viewing a DVD by Father Robert Barron called "Untold Blessings." In the second of three parts in this presentation, Father Barron talks about the wrath of God as it relates to sinners. However, he doesn't preach hell-fire and brimstone, which is what I always associated God's wrath with. Instead, Father Barron equates the wrath of God with God's incredible, passionate desire to set things right again.

It has been said that God hates sin but loves the sinner. On one level this made since to me (since I am a sinner and I hope God loves me in spite of that), but on another level, once sin is in a sinner, how can the two be separated? Doesn't a sinner who has sinned deserve punishment for every misstep he's made? And isn't that what the wrath of God points to—that if you sin, you will be punished and therefore, you'd better watch your step because one wrong move could spell damnation for eternity?

No, actually. That's not what the wrath of God points to at all. The wrath of God is God's extreme desire to set things right, His anger that His children have been hurt by the sins they themselves have committed. In short, He is angry with the sin, not with the sinner.

The second piece of this understanding came this afternoon when my children and I went to see *The Chronicles of Narnia: The Lion, The Witch, and the Wardrobe*. In the movie (as I'm sure in the book too although I've never read it), a young boy out of spite and hurt agrees to turn his brother and sisters over to the White Witch (think Satan with long hair and icicles). It soon becomes apparent to the boy, however, that he's made a terrible mistake. He sees the witch for who she really is, and he tries to escape. Through a series of events, he is indeed reunited with his brother and sisters after talking with the magical Lion king, Aslan.

All now seems well, until the White Witch shows up to claim her prize. According to the story, it is written that once a traitor has betrayed someone, he is now hers forever. The young boy is trapped, caught in a net of his own willfulness and hurt. Aslan, the Lion (a symbol for Christ) assesses the situation and requests a private conference with the Witch. When they re-emerge, a deal has been struck although at first, we are not privy to the details of the deal.

Soon, however, Aslan voluntarily leaves camp. The two sisters follow him, and then as he approaches the Witch's camp, the two girls hide and watch. It is on the Stone Table that Aslan gives himself in place of the boy. Aslan is beaten, sheered, tied up, and then sacrificed by the Witch. Thinking she has now defeated the only one who could conquer her, she sets out full of vengeance and hatred to destroy the rest of the residents of Narnia who are not on her side.

However, she never counted on the resurrection of Aslan (much the way, I'm sure, Satan didn't see the resurrection of Jesus coming either). When Aslan returns, he makes his entrance on the high arch of a cliff overlooking the scene where his troops are being slaughtered by the Witch and her minions. Aslan takes one sweeping look and lets out a roar that shakes the entire countryside.

Call it what you want—anger, passion, wrath—Aslan is downright furious at what evil is doing to his people after he sacrificed himself on their behalf, and in short order he rectifies the situation. Evil is vanquished, and the residents of Narnia who have been slaughtered in the battle are restored by the potion the smallest daughter was given that very much resembles blood.

It is a clear symbol that all it takes is one drop of the Blood of Christ for those who have fallen asleep to death to be resurrected with Him.

So, the wrath of God? Yes, it is very much a reality. In fact, He loves us much like a parent whose child comes in two hours after curfew without having called. The parent is understandably angry, but the anger is really more a result of the overwhelming fear of what could have happened to the child. So it is with God. He's angry because He loves us so much. However, He is not angry with us, He is angry for us—standing in the breech between our stupidly choosing evil and what evil wants to do to us because of our stupid choices.

In this context, God's wrath not only meshes perfectly with His love, it also suddenly becomes not scary but comforting. That He would love me so much that when I sin and Satan comes to drag my soul away into his bitter, hate-filled world, Jesus Christ steps in the middle and says, "No, take Me instead"—knowing full well that Satan cannot pass up a deal so sweet. In doing this, Christ ransomed my life by giving up His own. Now when Satan tries to take me out anyway, the passion of Christ and of God the Father is aroused and sets about to banish evil from whence it came. This is without a doubt the most poignant image of God's love for me that I could ever conceive of witnessing.

The wrath of God? It makes me feel more protected and loved than I ever thought possible. In fact, it's now one of the most joyous, emotionally overwhelming concepts I've ever encountered. Who would've thought? (2006)

The Keynote

Who are you tuned to? Are you tuned at all? Have you ever taken the time to get tuned or to decide what note you want to be tuned to?

In the life of an orchestra member these are serious questions. Imagine now yourself sitting with your instrument, preparing for your performance. You do a few scales to warm up, you angle your music stand toward the conductor, and then at the appointed moment, you play.

Now it is conceivable that you and every other member of that orchestra have spent literally hours and hours practicing for this performance. You have gone through every sequence hundreds of times—the tough ones a couple hundred. You know every fermata by heart and every trill by memory, and so do your fellow musicians.

However, in all your preparations, you forgot one very important fundamental detail. You forgot to tune up with the keynote player.

In an orchestra it goes like this: the keynote player sounds the keynote loud, long, and strong. Everyone else listens carefully and then plays the same note, then they tune up their instruments until the note from each instrument comes into perfect pitch with the key note. Then and only then can harmonious music emanate from the assembled players—no matter how many hours they have practiced.

So, who are you tuned to? Anyone? Have you taken the time to decide that Christ is your keynote player, or are you simply tuning to whomever happens to show up in your life? Or maybe you want to play your own pitch no matter what anyone else says. If so, may I ask you how well your performance is going?

Are you in harmony or discord with those around you? Your

family, friends, co-workers? Do you follow this one and then that one—splitting yourself between pitches, hoping somehow you'll sound right some of the time?

If so, may I suggest that taking some time to tune to the keynote may be the answer to your frenetic searching for the good, harmonious life. Seek Jesus out, let Him be your keynote player, tune yourself to Him, and watch harmony abound like never before. (2006)

The Joy of Grapefruit

We are once again approaching the great fruit lesson in my friend's Sunday School class, and she is really hoping that they leave something other than grapefruit this time. Let me explain.

Last year she came up with an innovative way to teach the fruits of the Holy Spirit and Holy Spirit Moments at the same time. The concept was simple. She got a variety of fruits—an apple, an orange, a banana, a grapefruit, and others. She put them all in a basket. At the end of class each student chose a fruit. Then on a tack board, my friend would reveal what fruit of the Holy Spirit that fruit represented.

Apple = kindness
Orange = patience
and so on.

Throughout the following week the students were to pay attention to the times and situations that either their fruit or their fruit of the Holy Spirit came up and report back to the class on these events the next Sunday.

Unfortunately there were not enough girls for all of the fruit. At the end, the grapefruit was still in the basket. Being the good sport she is, my friend decided to play along. She took the grapefruit. When the corresponding fruit of the Holy Spirit was revealed, she found out to her chagrin that she had "joy."

"Joy?" she asked me later. "Are you kidding me?" That's when the fun started. The next day she came home to find a basket of three grapefruits on her front porch. I was praying she liked grapefruit so she wouldn't throw them at me.

Amazingly it wasn't the grapefruit she was thrilled about—it was the basket. It was done in the exact colors she planned on redoing her kitchen in. She said, "How did you know?" Well, I didn't, but Somebody did.

At the time she was taking a full load of college classes and getting more and more overwhelmed. However, it soon became apparent there was joy all around her that she hadn't been noticing.

The word started popping up everywhere. In lectures, in reading, in conversation—there it would be: Joy. And it wasn't just her. Suddenly everywhere I went, someone was talking about joy. In songs, in commercials on the radio, on television—everywhere.

We laughed in amazement many times that week, and then came Friday. She asked my husband and me to go with her and a friend to the movies to see *Friday Night Lights*.

For those who don't know, this is a rough and tumble football movie. And "rough" is a good word. There's blood and dirty hits and players dealing with all manner of horrible situations in their personal lives.

By the end, predictably the team is down as they go into the locker room for the halftime pep talk by their coach, played by the extremely rough around the edges Billy Bob Thornton. That's when the fun began.

He's motivating his team by saying they should go out and do their best. That's when it happened. He said (paraphrase): If you go out there and play with *joy in your hearts* you've already won.

I don't know which of us was more stunned. She looked at me. I looked at her, and we both started laughing. You know that shaking kind of laughing when you can't actually laugh out loud. When one of us would get it together, the other would start shaking, and here we'd go again.

Thankfully the movie didn't last long after that, and presently we were back out in the hallway. She was like, "Can you believe that?" I said, "Yeah, joy in a football movie!"

Ah, the joy of grapefruit. Makes me wonder what "fruit" we're going to get this year. (2005)

The If-Only Mirage

There are some phrases that are quintessentially of the world. The very essence of them is borne in the ego-belief system which holds such detrimental beliefs as "I am separate," "I have to do it all on my own," "I must make God proud of me," "Success must look just this way, or it's not really success." Much like the idea that knowing how to compete will help us "get ahead," the if-only mirage sucks our time down a black hole and virtually guarantees our ultimate failure.

Although I have written about this phenomenon in vague sketches in my novels—such as when a heroine believes she could have a relationship with the hero "if only…" she was prettier, richer, more worldly, etc., it is only when the heroine STOPS the if only games that she really begins to live. In truth, how you end the "if only" thought rarely matters except in analyzing and understanding how destructive and paralyzing the phrase is.

Take my friend for example. She grew up with "if only" playing non-stop in her head. Nonetheless, in the last year or so, her reality has shifted dramatically. The more she puts her life in God's hands, the better life gets. And I mean demonstrably better not just in theory. At one time her "if-only" list included the following… If only I could find my own apartment… If only I could get me a car… If only I could get that part time job I want… If only I could join the small prayer group…

This afternoon I went to see said friend, and she said, "You know I realized this weekend how often I say 'if-only.' If only I was thinner. If only I made more money. If only I could find the love of my life. Then I started really hearing myself, and I thought, 'If Staci was here, what would she say?'"

She laughed because she's starting to hear my responses

without me even having to be there (in case you're perplexed, that's because it's really the Holy Spirit talking when I do because I've turned these types of discussions totally over to Him; therefore, in truth, I don't even need to be there. All she has to do is to look into her own heart and ask the Holy Spirit in her, and the answer will be there. The answer is not about me. It's about Him.)

Interestingly she added another fascinating insight right after that. She said, "But then, I started asking, then what? You know. If only this would happen, then... what? What would really change? What would really happen? Would I really be that much happier if I was still the same person and only that changed?"

This point is particularly important when the if-onlys begin to take hold of you and start playing on-loop in your brain. And then, of course there is if-onlys twin sister I wish... I wish I could go back and... I wish I could go back to August, I would do everything differently. I wish things had been different...

What these two phrases effectively do is keep you from *living right now*! "If only" basically says, "I can't live fully until *this* happens." If only I could find a man, then I could really live. So, of course, that means you can't fully live now because there's no man in sight. If only I could pay my bills, then I'd be happy. Which means you can't be happy now because the bills aren't paid. This sets up a dangerous trap because your ego has convinced you it's your fault, AND it's convinced you that there's no way you can experience happiness at this moment because this criteria has not been met.

Does this mean go out and party even if you can't pay your bills? No. The circumstance of not having money (or not having a man) is an opportunity to trust that God will provide (if you have truly given your life over to Him) and to be willing to allow His peace to come into you even though at this moment you can't see how this will work out. Remember: *We walk by faith and not by sight.*

Further, "if only" is an empty-promise because you know as well as I do that the second an if only happens, there are ten more standing there to take that particular one's place. If only I could meet the man of my dreams. Then you meet him. Oh, if only he would ask me to marry him. Then he does. Now, if only we can get married. The certificate is signed. If only we can find a house.

House arrives. If only he could find a new job, this one is stressing him out. He does. If only I could get that promotion. You do. If only I had more time off…

And on and on and on it goes keeping you from *ever* living right now.

I believe that if-only is the ego's way of keeping you from living this present moment by holding out the promise of what could be tomorrow. "I wish" is the ego's way of keeping you from living this present moment by holding a past mistake over your head. Either way, having these two destructive, paralyzing phrases on loop in your brain means *you are not living right now.*

So the question is: Are you waiting to start living in God's peace, joy, love, life, hope, and grace until you get all of the "if onlys" to work out, or are you willing to risk living right now— regardless of whether or not any of that stuff ever comes true—and see where that takes you?

Of course, that's a question only you can answer. (2006)

The GOOD News!
Feb. 26, 2007

I finally get it. Okay, it took me a while, but I finally understand why the Gospel is called "The Good News." This morning my church burned to the ground. Thankfully, the adjacent building was saved because of the awesome fire department, but the sanctuary is a total loss. At approximately 5:30 this morning the roof caved in, and everything that wasn't already destroyed by the fire was demolished. Interestingly as I sat and watched the building I have grown to so love burn to the ground, I couldn't help but be so grateful for The GOOD News I have learned there, and The GOOD News is this...

This is Friday, pure and simple. Friday was full of anguish and mourning as Christ carried that cross up the hill and was nailed there for all to see. It wouldn't have been good news if that had been the end. If that had been the end, suffering and mourning like today would have been all we could have done. That would have been anything but good news.

Ah! But that wasn't the end, and thus it is truly The GOOD News! Because of the gift given us by our Gracious and Loving God, we know... we KNOW that even in the depths of the pain of Friday... Sunday's coming. Sunday, the Resurrection, Christ glorified is coming! And so even in the midst of sorrow for the old, even in the midst of the pain of saying good-bye to what was, we know that what is coming is infinitely better than we ever could have imagined! Now, let me tell you, on a day like today, THAT is GOOD News!

So, if you are suffering through a Friday in your life. If yet another bill has found its way into your mailbox, if yet again you haven't made the sales you had hoped, if yet again you are left to mourn what appears to be the death of your dream... TAKE HOPE! Take JOY! Rejoice! Because The Good News says, "This is only Friday. You must let Friday die so that Sunday can live, and never ever forget that Sunday's coming! That's right all you toilers who think 'What's the use?' The use is SUNDAY'S COMING, and it's going to be better than you can even imagine!"

What a day, God. What a day! (2006)

The Gift of Prayer

Don Chapman once said, "Pray as you can; don't pray as you can't." How do you pray? There was a time that I prayed as fast as I could so I could get on to more exciting things. I knew I should pray, but it was a should, a have to, not a want to.

I felt guilty for not praying more, but prayer felt so stilted to me—a bunch of words that helped me gain favor with an Almighty God who had to be appeased with the right words at the right time or else.

Oh, how wrong I was. Granted, I looked pretty good at praying. I went to church every week and knew every prayer "by heart" which is ironic because very few of them actually made it all the way to my heart.

What I didn't understand back then is that prayer can give you a freedom that nothing else can, but not the way I used to do it.

Brennan Manning in *The Ragamuffin Gospel* says, "Prayer is another area that many people struggle with because they aren't aware that in the freedom of the Spirit, there are as many ways of praying as there are individual believers."

That was my first mistake—judging my prayer by what others said you had to do. I am a cradle Catholic. I grew up on the rosary. There's nothing wrong with the rosary, unless you pray it like I used to.

"Our Father, Who art in Heaven... I wonder how long this is going to take... Hail Mary, full of grace... did I switch beads that last time? I don't remember. I'm not sure I did... Hail Mary, full of grace... do we have three more to go or four...Hail Mary, full of grace... ugh, how much longer?"

It was *horrible*. One night I was at a retreat. I'd been in the Spirit all day, and then we started the rosary. I tried. I really did. For two whole decades I tried to pray like I was supposed to, beads in hands, head bowed, thoughts tuned only to Him. But I couldn't do it. Finally, fed up with myself for not being able to pray "right," I put the beads down, just laid them right in front of where I sat. Then I started praying my way.

As I prayed, I did the other part of prayer I had learned—I turned on my side of the walkie-talkie. You see, I think that prayer is not only or even primarily about us talking to God. It is more about opening ourselves so that He can talk to us.

And talk He did. As the prayers continued around me and even through me, He began to talk, and I began to cry. They were tears of healing, more than that, they were tears of unspeakable gratefulness and joy for all He has done in my life, for His grace, for His love, but most of all for Him.

"Pray as you can; don't pray as you can't."

Listen for Him speaking to you as you pray, pray the way you pray, and prayer will be something you never again do because you have to. (2006)

Especially Now

There are times in life that stress isn't even the right word. I was having one of those times. My wonderful, awesome brother had been taken to the mental hospital, and nothing was making any sense in what had once been what I considered my life. I had thought of many ways my life might go. This was not one of them.

For anyone who's ever had a close family member fall prey to mental illness, you know that when things get out-of-whack in their world, yours starts making less and less sense as well. Things you took for granted are no longer reliable. Things that seemed so obvious before suddenly look totally different, and there is no way to get them into logical order.

I knew Raef had been struggling. I had known for quite some time. But the mental hospital? That just was so out of anything I could've imagined so as to be surreal. But he was there, and not going was out of the question. So I headed there. Now I didn't know how in the world I would ever be able to walk into that place—what would I say? What could I say? What would it be like? What would he be like?

In the midst of the swirling questions, I reached for the One constant in my life—my Savior and my Friend. "God, I don't know about this. I really don't. Am I supposed to trust you even now?"

It seemed such a simple question, and it had an even simpler answer.

Patiently, lovingly the answer came back to me. "No. Not even now… especially now."

Since that day I've had a lot of Especially Now moments.

There are many things I do not understand about this life—why things happen, why they happen to who they happen to, what to do when horrible things happen to wonderful people in our lives. What

I do know is that in those most confusing of moments, we have a friend who is holding out his hands and whispering, "Trust Me... especially now." (2007)

The Four Parts of a Blessing

One of the stories in the Bible that always fascinated me was the story of the small boy who had five loaves and two fish. Can you imagine being that kid? His mother, I'm sure, packed his lunch for him that morning. "Now, be careful with this. Don't smash that bread, and no trading with anybody!" So, off he goes to see this guy they call Jesus.

Jesus talks, and then it's time to eat. Think about this, there were 5,000 men there—which may mean there were many more than that when you count the women and the children—*and no one thought to bring anything to eat except this one kid*! Okay, this is not Kansas City, Missouri. There isn't a McDonald's five blocks down from the convention center where Jesus is speaking. They are out in the middle of the country, and they came out here with no food.

I think it's quite possible the people who came to hear Jesus speak may not have realized that's where they were headed that day. Maybe they were headed further down the road to work or coming back from visiting someone. They saw this crowd and thought, "Hmm, wonder what's going on over there." So, they pulled the camel over and went to see what was up.

They didn't intend to stay so long. They had fully intended to only stay a minute or two to see what was happening. But Jesus was a dynamic speaker. I'm quite sure He was a dynamic spirit—one of those people that you're just drawn to and you can't really explain why. So, He's teaching, and they're listening, and the crowd is growing. Then all of a sudden one of the disciples realizes, "Hey, man, we haven't eaten in like hours!"

So, he goes up to Jesus and says, "Tell these people to go home. We need to go get something to eat." To which, Jesus turns to him and says, "Feed them yourself."

Okay, I've been to enough "community events." As the day winds down, if you've had a good day, the meat is running a bit thin, we're out of potatoes, and I really hope we don't get many more people coming in. These things go through a person's mind when they are in charge. I'm quite sure they went through this disciple's mind as well.

But Jesus said to feed the people, so what do they do? The only thing they can do... They start looking around for any food available. That's when one of the disciples sees this boy. With very few other options, they ask him for his lunch. Probably knowing his mother will be mad but seeing little other choice, he gives them the food he has.

You know the rest of the story. Jesus takes the meager offering, blesses it, has it distributed, and it feeds the multitude. This is exactly how the blessings in our lives work if we understand what really happened here.

The boy most likely did not make that bread himself, nor did he make the fish. He was given them—by his mother, yes—but even more so by his Heavenly Father. They were his blessing. Now he could've kept that blessing to himself, but he didn't. When he was asked, he gave his blessing away. He gave that blessing to Jesus. Jesus took the blessing that had been given the boy, blessed it, and it was distributed as a blessing to all those present.

Think about what Jesus is calling us to do through this story with the blessings and talents in our own lives. He has given them to us, and we can keep them to ourselves if we wish. But I think He is inviting us to see what can happen when we don't keep them to ourselves. When we give them back to Him and let Him bless them, and then we share them with the world. It becomes not two fish and a few loaves of bread—a small, hardly-worth-mentioning offering—it becomes "enough to feed a multitude." And there are even 12 baskets leftover.

Yes, we can keep our talents and blessings to ourselves. We can hold them close to our hearts and hoard them so that they don't slip through our fingers. However, consider how incredible that blessing could become if we give it back to Jesus, let Him bless it, and then let Him, through us, use it to improve the world around us.

It's something to think about. (2005)

Making a Quilt

A friend was having trouble understanding how life works when you're eating only from the Tree of Life, when God steps in and does it for you. She had never learned the great gift of surrender or what Jesus truly meant when He said, "Come to Me all you who labor and are burdened, and I will give you rest."

So I put it to her using the following metaphor.

Surrendering to God is like this:

A quilt needs to be made. It is a special quilt, for a birthday present for a very special person in your life. Your best friend is an expert quilt maker. She has made quilts all her life and has won many awards for her quilt-making abilities. She also can make quilts very cheaply because she simply makes them out of the scraps she already has. She can also make them very fast because she knows what she's doing.

Now, you have three choices: 1) Make the quilt yourself without asking for her help. 2) Make it yourself with her helping you. 3) Let her make it.

If you choose #1, you've got a steep learning curve, it will be much more expensive because you will have to buy the books, material, thread, and maybe even a sewing machine. It will also be more time consuming. You probably will not win any awards for the quilt, nor will you break any speed records. But you will know that YOU DID IT.

If you choose #2, you will at least have help on the tough spots. When you don't know what to do next because the bobbin got caught in the feeder, you will have someone to call to ask, "How do you do this?" Still, it will be expensive because you will have to buy your own material, thread, and possibly even a sewing machine—unless you borrow hers. You probably will not win any awards with it. And it will definitely take up quite a bit of your time. Yet you will know that YOU DID IT.

(I can here the positive thinkers of the world lining up and cheering you on now!)

However, you also have the option of choosing #3. You can let her do it. Doing this, you will know several things from the outset: The quilt will be done right. There won't be any dropped stitches or batting sticking out where it shouldn't be. It will be done with the least expense possible. It will be done quickly (because your friend doesn't procrastinate like you do). It will be absolutely beautiful. And you will know that YOU DID NOT DO IT. But they will still say, "Thank YOU." They won't thank her.

(Unbelievable that I would even suggest such a thing, I know.)

Here's the thing. You have grown out of #1. This would be the legalism that you have pointed out you are no longer a slave too. However, you are trapped in #2. You are doing it and asking God to bless what YOU do. Hate to tell you this, but it doesn't work that way. The only things that are truly Holy are those things that GOD does.

Let's take a couple Biblical examples:

The little boy with the loaves and fishes. He had the loaves and fishes, but he did not keep them and try to multiply them on his own. *He gave them to God and let God feed the people.* He was securely in #3. Why? Because he knew he couldn't do it, so he let God have his "talents" and let God do it through him.

How about Lazarus? Yeah. There's a case. He was wrapped in death cloth, stuck a tomb, dead for four days. No way could he have done anything much less got up and walked on his own. Yet, he didn't have to. He let God do it for him. He just took the steps Jesus called him to take.

And then there's Peter, walking on the water. Do you really think Peter is the one who did that? I'll give you a hint. When he looked down at the waves and away from Jesus, he sank. Why? Because he realized, "What do I think I'm doing? I can't do this!"

That's right. He can't. I can't. You can't. But GOD can…if we let Him. (2006)

The Fence

We had just been talking about it. Not ten minutes before we were talking about what place God's rules should play in your life. Are they "in stone" so that God has something to point to when He throws you into the fire? "You should've known! I gave you the Ten Commandments, and you did it anyway!"

We had discussed our children and whether or not you can teach a child with "only love," or do you have to pound the rules into them? How will they know what's right and wrong if you don't set down the rules and make sure the child knows what they are? That was the question. Don't you need the rules to raise a child?

In the discussion I said what I've said in other articles, that God gave us the Ten Commandments because He loves us. He knows that there are times when we are so in the fog of "right now" that we, if left to our own experiences and understanding, might fall into mistakes that will forever alter our lives for the worse. He knows, and so He gave us a way to know "this is not done if you want to live a healthy, prosperous, successful life." So the rules are there not for punishment, but for love.

Shortly after our discussion, I walked outside to go to my vehicle, which was parked a considerable distance down the road. We were on the far outskirts of the town. There was very little ambient light from about a half-mile away. In short, it was dark out there. I was in a hurry, so I didn't wait for my eyes to adjust. I stepped off the porch and walked out to the parked cars.

Not familiar with the lay of the land, I strode past the cars. Trying to figure out how I could get to my van without walking on the road—although there were no cars there anyway, I kept walking. I tried to see where I was going, figure out where I was even as I kept walking. Finally, my brain said, "Just find the road and then follow it to the van."

It's interesting how in the fog of "right now" my brain works. It keeps talking to me, trying to discern where I am, where I'm going, how I'm going to get there even as I keep going. Very rarely does it say, "Hey! Stop and figure it out before we go forward!" Oh, no. We're going, and we've got to get there now.

Then I realized that my feet were brushing weeds. "Oh, it's the weeds. I'm in the ditch. The road should be right here…" Suddenly I found myself standing six inches from A FENCE! Not just any fence. This was a four level, barbed-wire, held together with metal stand-up fence posts fence. In less than a heartbeat, I stopped my headlong motion. I literally said, "A fence? What's a fence doing on this side of the road?"

Yes, I'm not always the brightest bulb in the lamp. Then I turned around and realized with some chagrin that I had gone past the cars, through one ditch, onto and over the road, down and back up the other ditch, and I didn't figure out my mistake… until I suddenly saw that fence.

Funny, I think that's exactly the lesson we were just talking about minutes before. (2005)

The Anchor

God has a sense of humor. That much I know. He will put things in my path, make me wonder what's going on, and then reveal it in a way that is totally WOW! It's happened many times over the years. One of the coolest times was when I went on a retreat. My husband had been on retreat already, and he brought home a cross made in the shape of an anchor. Now this retreat was one that "some things are meant to be secret until you go."

I liked the anchor/cross, and I wanted to ask, but I thought it better to learn what it meant for myself. When I went on retreat, one of my first missions was to find out what that anchor meant. The first night came and went... no anchor. The next morning, I got ready for this great story about the anchor. Nothing. By lunchtime, I was seriously frustrated. Still nothing about an anchor.

Then they brought a banner in to announce the next event. There was an anchor on the bottom of it! I just knew I was going to find out what it meant. But the event proceeded and ended. Nothing. Ugh.

I looked across at one of my tablemates, and she had anchor earrings and anchors on her blouse. Now when this type of thing happens (the message coming through someone who couldn't be in on it), I know it's a God thing not just a man thing. So, I started paying more attention. Another of my tablemates read a little verse from the uplifting jar of verses.

One of the team members was standing close. She came over and said, "Oh, that's by (I don't remember her name). She was an *anchorite* nun."

I about started laughing. So I was like, "Okay, what's up God? I know You're talking just to me here. What do You want to tell me?"

It took until the next event to find out. We were sitting in the chapel, and all was quiet. I took out my notebook to record some of the things that had happened. As I was writing, I said, "Okay, God, what's up with the anchor?"

He said, "Draw it."

Having been in these types of conversations enough to know you don't argue, I did as I was told. I drew an anchor.

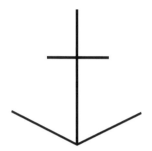

"Draw it again. What do you see?"

"Well, the cross. That's easy. Okay. Cool God."

"No, there's more. Draw it again."

I drew it again. The cross first and then the bottom piece—down and up. Down and up. I just kept tracing over it, asking Him. "What is it?" A smiley face?

"No. Look at it."

"It's... What is it? It's a... bridge!"

Then I saw it clearly. It was a bridge as if over a chasm. "Cool, God."

"There's more."

"More? Okay." So I drew it really slowly. Until I realized, the left part of the bridge dropped *until it connected with the cross.*

"Ah, now you're getting it."

So we drop until we grab onto the cross. Again, awesome!

Then I realized that wasn't all. There was a part beyond the cross, a part that led back up. "What's this part, God?"

"It's when *you* let go, and start trusting Me to hold you up."

Sometimes the simplest of lessons is so profound that it takes your breath away. That's what this one was for me.

I saw it then. On the left bank is Fear, and you fall into the fear until you grab onto the cross. You will hang over that chasm for as long as you need to. You hold the cross as long as you believe you need to. But if you're lucky, you begin to realize that it's not you holding on at all. It's Him.

When you let go and begin to trust Him, He will gently bring you up to the other shore of Peace.

Fear to Peace.
Frustration to Patience.
Hatred to Love
Despair to Hope
Sin to Grace
Anger to Joy

If you are falling, grab onto the cross. If you've been hanging onto the cross, thinking you have to do it or you will fall, release your grip and trust Him to hold you up.

It is the coolest way to live ever!   (2007)

The Evidence of Things Not Seen

A friend of mine was recently lamenting about her difficulties losing weight. I could sympathize as that challenge is in my life as well. She said, "It's just so hard when you do this stuff like eating healthy, but you don't see any progress. I just want to say, 'God, why is this not working?'"

Not only do I understand her frustration in that area, I have the same challenge in my writing. I'm following, doing and working, but where is the evidence that this is going to get me where I want to go or where He has in mind for me to go?

The hilariously sad thing is this same friend recently sent me a story she had written that plainly stated: "Faith is the substance of things hoped for and the evidence of things not seen." So it's not like she didn't know. I reminded her of that, and she said, "Yeah...?" as if she didn't see the connection.

What you need, I told her, is to keep the faith that each little thing you do toward your goal each day will eventually get you where you want to be. The problem is that we don't just want evidence, we want daily and sometimes hourly evidence that what we're doing is working.

For example, let's say you want to lose 25 pounds. You start out with the best of intentions. You're really doing well, sticking to your healthy diet and exercising. For three solid weeks you are the model of a champion, and what do you know? It works. You lose six whole pounds. You're feeling great. This is going to work.

Then in the fifth week reality sets in. You've been exercising and eating right but you find you've actually gained a pound! What's this? How can this be? You've been breaking your neck, and you've gained weight?

Well, what's the use, right? Why work, why do this if it's

pointless? And so, what happens? We quit. We give up. Why? Because there is no evidence that this is working, and by golly, *we want evidence* or what's the point?

If I've deprived myself all day, if I've exercised for an hour, eaten baked chicken and steamed vegetables (instead of that fried chicken and potato salad I really wanted), then I want to see some evidence NOW that this is working.

There may be no greater example than weight loss, unless it's my book sales. I told my friend, "It's like this week. On Saturday I sold 35 books. Woohoo! But now it's Thursday, and I'm bummed because I haven't sold anything since." What happened to my excitement from Saturday?

It's like I don't just want evidence, I want on-going, continuous evidence!

O, me of little faith. I really need to work on trusting that what I'm doing is working—when there is evidence and when there is not, understanding that is precisely when I need faith the most. For if our faith is based on evidence, it's not really faith at all.

Faith is the substance of things hoped for and the evidence of things not seen—like this is working, there is a point, keep it up, and it's all going to be worth it. That's faith. (2006)

The Blessings of Being Poor in Spirit

Okay, in our world today, poor is not exactly something to aspire toward. More often "poor" is something you fall into through misfortune and bad luck. You don't climb the ladder to be poor. You don't compete and learn and practice to be poor. No, poor is not an aspiration. It is a curse—or so it would seem.

It might come as a huge shock to you when I say we are indeed to aspire to be poor. Poor in spirit that is. Yes, the first of the Beatitudes is as relevant today as it was when Jesus stood on the Mount. In fact, it may be more relevant now.

Let me for a moment describe what it means to NOT be poor in spirit. You will have to learn all the rules of the world and how to break them. You will forever have to watch your back for one of the greatest characteristics of being on top is that someone younger, smarter, more powerful, more ruthless is waiting one rung down to knock you off.

When you are NOT poor in spirit, you can rely on only one person—yourself. All others playing this game are out only for themselves, and you would do well to remember that. This is an especially important point to remember when they begin to build you up.

In *Star Wars: Revenge of the Sith*, the chancellor (think the snake in the garden with nice clothes) tells Anikan, "It is clear you are the best one for the job." And later, "They are jealous of your power." Now if you think the chancellor was being benevolent in his compliments, think again.

In the Garden of Eden, the serpent used a similar ploy. "God knows if you eat it, you will be just like Him…" What he is saying is, "Look, you too can be a god. You can have power. You can have all of this if you'll just…." Again we hear this enticement when

Satan tempts Jesus, "You can have all of this…"

The moment you turn to yourself as your power, you have turned against the idea of being poor in spirit. I have done this many times. When I tried to learn the ways of marketing and selling and being "good enough to get published." This is the trap I was falling into. When I listened to others tell me I had to sell X number of books before I would be considered published, I was again in this trap. Why? Because I was trying to prove my own worth, and I was using the world's definitions as my yardstick.

Let me tell you as one who's been there—it's no place to live!

I heard a preacher who substituted the word "lucky" for "blessed." How lucky are the poor in spirit. How lucky are you if you know and admit that you're not all it.

If your worth is wrapped up in power, what happens when the wheel of fortune inevitably turns? Who are you when they get a new go-to guy? To the world which exalts you, you are expendable. But to the One who allows you to be nothing for your own sake, you will be exalted. "The last shall be first and the first, last."

When you know your place is not at the head of the table, when you see that your faults are unforgivable, when you know you can't do it yourself, *only then* do you lay yourself down at His feet and beg for mercy.

You're not saying, "Lord, I have earned your forgiveness." Rather you are on your face in the dust *knowing* you do not deserve His mercy, but you are begging for it anyway. You are a helpless child who can do nothing for themselves but have learned to raise your hands to the Father and trust that He will pick you up, love you just as you are, and in His grace and faithfulness have mercy on you and take care of you.

This is what it means to be poor in spirit. That you have seen where going on your own power gets you and it's no place that you ever want to be again.

The blessings of the poor in spirit?

Honesty about how small you are and about how much you need Him.

A disregard for your own plans and self in exchange for His plans and His life.

A blessed release (relief) that you don't have to know all the answers because you know the One who does, and you trust that He will do it all in His time, in His way, for the good of all those who love Him (and that includes you!).

These are but some of the blessings of being poor in spirit, and when you find them, the Kingdom of Heaven will be yours because the powers of this world will no longer have any hold on you, and that, my friend, is Heaven! (2006)

Prophets

I've always heard the term, "you are baptized priest, prophet, and king." I don't honestly know if this is just a Catholic phrase or not, but I've heard it at every baptism I've ever been to, which could easily stretch into the hundreds. But I'd never really thought about it. One evening in my hometown parish, the priest was talking about prophets of the Old Testament. He said how hard their lives were, how they spoke about God and people threw them out for their determination to speak God's Word no matter what.

John the Baptist, the greatest prophet of them all, was beheaded. Not exactly a fate I want. However, the truth is, we are baptized priest, prophet, and king. The priest then asked, "Who have you been a prophet for this week?" I didn't call it that way at the time, but immediately, I saw all the discussions about Christ and His love I'd had during the previous week. Friends, family members, my newsletter, other writers... There are very few conversations I have that don't end up with a "Wow. That was a good one, Holy Spirit."

Furthermore, of the three in the Trinity, I have a special friendship with the Holy Spirit. For example, recently my computer CD burner went on the fritz. It had to be changed, and although I asked four other people, there was no one available to help me. Now, I'm good with words. I am not good with appliances, motors, and certainly not computers components! But it had to be changed, and it had to be changed that day. So I disconnected everything and took a deep breath.

All the while I worked, I sang, "Holy Spirit, fill me with Your peace..." changing the last word to whatever I needed at the moment... wisdom, ability, grace, knowledge. After about thirty minutes of this, my oldest daughter asked, "Why do you keep singing the Holy Spirit song?" I said, "Because I know I'm not the one who is going to get this done!" So, me and the Holy Spirit are pretty tight.

Just after talking about how we are prophets for others, the priest then turned the idea around. "And who has been a prophet for you this week?" I think the tears came instantly because I know the list did. My mom, my sister, Betty, Susan, Deb, Stefani, Kayla, Andrew, Damian…. There were people on the 'net and people who are my readers. There were people I hadn't seen in a very long time, and people that I talk with three and four times a day. Lines of them, all pointing me in the direction God most wanted me to go that week—including the priest giving the sermon!

The sermon ended, and we stood for the Nicene Creed. Now, in my defense, I admit that I'm weird. I'm probably the only person on the planet who cries if I pay attention to the words of that list of beliefs. By the second line, tears are generally streaming down my face as I see how very blessed and fortunate I am to have a God Who loves me so much that He would choose to reveal Himself so plainly.

Then I got to this line:

"We believe in the Holy Spirit, the Lord, the Giver of life, Who proceeds from the Father and the Son. With the Father and Son, He has been worshipped and glorified. *He has spoken through the prophets.*"

It was a full five minutes before I could get another word out of my mouth! Here it was. In plain language. Written millenniums ago! The Holy Spirit has spoken through the prophets. Now, until that night I had always interpreted that line to mean: Isaiah, Jeremiah, Ezekiel… and it does. But it also means my mom, my sister, Betty, Susan, Deb…

What a gift! To not just know it, but to SAY it and be thankful every week for the prophets in my life who have brought God to me, who have spoken for Him, who have acted for Him to teach me the lessons I most need to know!

Sometimes, there is just no doubt in my mind how much God loves me. It makes me cry. (2006)

Projections

Boy, we can get ourselves into some real messes, you know that? And when I say "we," I mean WE. Me included. We set things up in our lives and things are set up in our lives that drag us down into the muck. In reaching for the things we want, those things we think we need in order to live, we make rotten decisions and let people do rotten things toward us sometimes to the point that we think there is no way out.

I read today in Max Lucado's *Traveling Light* about the man in the jungle. He's gotten separated from his group. He's lost his equipment. He has no idea how to get out, and all he has left to do is sit on a tree stump and cry. Now that's a pretty good picture of some of us. We are so far down in the muck, any sane person would conclude there is no way out, sit down on the stump, and cry.

A friend of mine recently shared her story with me, and as the details piled up, it was pretty clear she'd been in the muck for a long time. She hadn't told anyone other than her therapist because she was afraid of judgment, condemnation, and ridicule. Aren't we all? So, we stuff all the bad down, hoping it will go away, praying it won't try to find us. Yet it does. It has radar for our weak moments.

It torments us at night and is always there in the back of our minds, playing like an annoying record that we can't shut off. "Sure, they like you now, but they wouldn't if they only knew." After the discussion with my friend, I got to thinking about how God relates to our Muck Time, and how He would have us relate to it.

If I could go back now, I would ask my friend, "If you had gone all the way down and done the horrible things you were thinking of doing, would God have loved you any less?" Remarkably the answer is "No." God loves us. Period. He forgave us. Period. Does that give us license to go out and do every horrible thing in the book? Of course not. In fact, when we really get how much He loves us, our one and only goal becomes to love Him back to the very best of our ability. So God would not love you any less even if you did the horrible things you wanted to do.

But consider this: "If you had gone all the way down and done the horrible things you were thinking of doing, would you have loved you any less?" I think the obvious answer is, "Yes." We ourselves are the ones who hold the club of condemnation and shame. We believe we don't deserve good things because look at what we've done. We heap shame and reproach onto ourselves, putting on sack clothes of guilt and criticism. Remorse in its place is justified. Self-flogging is not.

The truth is we take our own thoughts about ourselves and our failings and we project them onto God. "He cannot love me—how could He? I don't even love me. I'm a horror to look at, a pathetic worthless inconsequential sinner." In the words of the song "Amazing Grace," I am a wretch.

But the words of that song are where our hope lies. "Amazing Grace, how sweet the sound that saved a wretch like me." God's grace, God's mercy, and yes, God's unfailing love are where our hope lies.

Looking at ourselves through the eyes of the world, we will invariably see wretchedness, sin, strife, hurt, loathing, grief, cowardice, avarice, culpability, and guilt. There is no way we can't for that is what we are. But that is not all we are. We are also sinners saved by grace. We didn't save ourselves. We couldn't. We are saved by grace—no matter how horrible we've been.

God's love trumps all. It always has. It always does. Let Him forgive you. Let Him love you. That's all He wants to do. (2006)

Pride or Gratefulness

The first deadly sin is pride. I knew that, but I could never figure out what I was supposed to feel when a project went well or the thing I'd worked for came to me. I battled this paradox for 36 years—until last night actually. It's amazing to me the lessons God is allowing me to learn through others. The more we talk about real things—God, His love, our mistakes and triumphs.

A very dear friend of mine and I were talking about how things have always gone well for him and how in the last few months, things have seemed to fall apart. He's been in a pretty desperate place, which I knew. He's battling years of programming that taught us both to work hard, dream big, and do what needed to be done to make it happen.

Now he was very good at this. Very good. And that's a large part of the problem. My descent in this area looked more like a gentle curve downward; his looks like a plunge off a cliff. As he struggles to work through the shards of the life he thought he was building, his confusion centers around why things went so wrong.

To him, it's because he made a decision he regretted. Okay, but that's not all of it. It's deeper and more profound than that. On a physical level he made a decision that he now sees will take years to pay off. He sees how what he thought was his dream is encroaching on his family's ability to get to their dreams because of the money he spent on his dream. And he wants with everything in him to go back to who he was, back to being able to make decisions and not worry about them, back to doing the right thing on his own.

I understand because I've been there. When I was marketing my books after they were published, I fell into the same trap. I worked and worked. I made decisions and then questioned those decisions. I became frustrated with the amount of time I was taking from my family, but I could see no other way around it. I had to sell those books. It was my responsibility. I made the decision to buy them, and I had to find a way to sell them.

That's what pride will do to you. Pride becomes your god. You will do anything to succeed so you can be proud of yourself (or at least not miserable and frustrated). And when you get there, you will do anything to keep that which you are so proud of. Granted, the longer you live, the more things this encompasses and the harder it gets to not lose.

Pride plunges you to depths that may have been unimaginable. It will make you do things you are not at all proud of, and it will hold you a prisoner of want and lack. Because no matter how much you have, someone else always has more, and to keep up, you will do some very dumb things.

So, what was the answer to my question of what to feel when things go right, when you get the thing you've worked so hard for? Ironically, my friend gave me the answer. He said, "I wanted to call and tell you thank you." Thank you. Gratefulness. A recognition that what happened was a gift.

God gives His children blessings, and this is very different than you getting whatever it is on your own. The less you rely on yourself, the less you puff yourself up with pride in your accomplishments, your abilities, and the material things you have acquired, the more you realize you didn't do it. He did. It was a gift.

Pride is an empty lie. It is a trick, which will leave you lying under the bus of failure—no matter how high you go. A story that opened my eyes to this lesson is Garth Brooks and his deal with Wal-Mart in 2005. After selling over 100 million albums over his career, he went to his record label because Wal-Mart had approached him to put together a compilation box set of his last six albums.

Hearing the story, I was thinking, "Wow! Everybody wins. What a deal." Then came the kicker. The record label turned him down *because they didn't think he could sell 250,000 copies*! He'd sold 100 *million* and now they didn't think they could break even because he wouldn't sell enough copies.

Okay, I don't know if you've ever listened to country music in your life, but let me tell you, that is a kick in the teeth if I've ever heard one. I honestly don't know how they kept a straight face while they told the top selling artist of all time, "We don't think anybody wants to buy your stuff anymore."

That's what pride and being inflated on your own abilities will get you. That's what the world will do to you every single time. When you are succeeding for them, they will build you up, but the second they sense weakness or that you are no longer "on top," you're gone. No matter who you are.

On the other hand, when you hold your accomplishments loosely, knowing they are from God and that they are a gift, you can be so grateful for them when they come your way, and you can let them go just as easily. You can be grateful (as I am now) for every sale because you know you didn't do it, He did.

Case in point, I have a book signing coming up that I literally did very little to get to happen. A new reader friend of mine was so excited about my books, she wanted me to come for a signing. I haven't done a signing in several years. I don't even remember my last one. I'm sure I worked hard to get it to happen, and I'm sure I sold a few books. Beyond that, I couldn't tell you much about it.

But this upcoming signing is very different. Flyers are being handed out, not by me but by my friend who is inviting everyone she knows. She set it up with the bookstore. She went to the community paper to get a story in there. She went to the radio station to set up community service announcements. And one thing is for sure, I may sell one book, but I will be very grateful for that sale because I know… I didn't do this. He did!

So, who sold that last widget from your inventory? You, or Him? It's a good question to ask. (2006)

Of Waterpots and New Wine

And on the third day there was a wedding in Cana of Galilee, and the mother of Jesus was there; and Jesus was also invited, and His disciples, to the wedding. And when the wine gave out, the mother of Jesus said to Him, "They have no wine." And Jesus said to her, "Woman, what do I have to do with you? My hour has not yet come." His mother said to the servants, "Whatever He says to you, do it." Now there were six stone waterpots set there for the Jewish custom of purification... John 2: 1-6

There is more of course, but for our purposes we will stop right there. You've probably heard this story more times than you can count. It is of course the story of Jesus' first miracle when He changed water into wine. And not just any wine, no, the best wine. That lesson is for another article, for now I want to focus on the final eleven words of this passage.

Specifically I want to ask you to reread the passage and look closely at what kind of pots they used. In my previous reading of this passage, I had always pictured... well, pitchers. Large earthenware vessels that look like modern day vases. You know the kind you would normally put wine into. But that's NOT what it says! NO. They put it in "stone waterpots set there for the Jewish custom of purification." In the Message Bible it says it this way... "six stone pots, used by the Jews for ritual washings..." Do you know what that means?

Very simply, those pots were used to enforce and carry out the rules, the law, the prescribed way of purifying yourself so you were clean enough to be presentable to society. Ritual washings were one of the biggest outward signs that someone was steeped in the rules of the Jews. There was a prescribed amount of time you had to wash, a prescribed amount of times you had to wash... And Jesus used *those* pots to do something totally *new*!

On top of that, the ritual washings were meant to show one's attempt to wash their sin away and thus be pure (If I wash myself enough, if I follow all of the rules, I shall be clean in the eyes of God). But the reality was, people were still dirty. Their bodies were dirty. Their hands were dirty. Their lives were dirty with sins they could not get rid of no matter how many times they washed themselves. And even when they washed, they got dirty again and thus had to wash again.

And Jesus (isn't He awesome?) used the pots that had been used to *wash* people, pots that symbolize us and our lives (dirty and nasty) to put *drinking wine* in. That is not just a little inconsequential detail! That's *huge*!

In fact, upon closer reading, it does not even say that Jesus first said, "Take those waterpots and wash them out, clean them out, and *then* fill them." No. He said, "Go and fill them." In all the times you have read and heard this passage, have you ever for a second pictured those servants as taking the time to go and wash out the pots on their own?

I haven't because prior to really reading this, I hadn't seen the need for them to. However, at the risk of your lunch, consider what they did. Guests had washed themselves in these pots. We don't know how many guests there were, but I have always pictured a rather large contingent of guests. At very least we know of fourteen, Jesus, the disciples, and Mary. At minimum, that's 28 hands, four for each pot, that have recently been washed in them. Now, Jesus says, "Go and fill those with water," and presumably without the benefit of Dawn Dishwashing Liquid, these pots were filled with water.

Then Jesus said, "Draw some out now, and take it to the headwaiter."

Something tells me, if I was one of those servants, I wouldn't have had the guts to tell the headwaiter what kind of receptacles that wine came from. Of course, we all know that the headwaiter proclaimed that this wine was the finest of wines.

So, consider that in one moment, Christ took us, these waterpots, empty yes, but permanently stained with the dirt of many hands. We had been steeped in the myth that our own actions could somehow wash us clean enough to gain entrance into Heaven. He took these empty, dirty, disgusting waterpots, and He poured Himself (His blood—water made wine) into us, and then *he did something new*! Not just new wine. The BEST wine! Not the rules. Not our sins. Him. And He is enough to make us THE BEST!

Believe me, I will never mistake those waterpots for pitchers again, nor will I so easily take for granted the mercy and grace He poured into me, dirty from within with no hope to ever get myself clean enough to earn anything. He did not require me to clean up before He washed me with Himself. He didn't look at me and say, "Ew, disgusting. Let's use something else."

Instead, He looked at me and saw not what I had done and what I was, He looked at what He could do for me, in me. That's the new wine—what He can do in a life, and trust me, it's the best thing you've ever tasted, poor dirty waterpot that you were before He showed up. (2006)

Love and Dust

I've been a Catholic all my life, so at present I've personally heard the Ash Wednesday admonishment 37 times. As the ashes are placed on your forehead, you are told, "Remember you are dust and to dust you shall return."

About three weeks ago, I was writing a book, and the character remembered what her grandmother used to tell her: "Remember you are love and to love you shall return."

When I went to Ash Wednesday Mass, I thought about these two sayings and wondered how can one be true if the other is also. Did I have to disregard the first's warning in order to embrace the second? All day long I thought about it, and finally it dawned on me what God was telling me through these two sayings.

Too many of us on this earth believe that what we do is important. We strive to "make a difference" in our world. We pursue educations and then jobs so that what we do will matter. Unfortunately, we're missing the point.

It is not what we do that matters at all. It's what He already did. The day that Christ carried my sins up Calvary's mountain, allowed Himself to be nailed to a tree, bled, suffered and died for me—that's what matters, and in truth, that's all that matters. Whether I get my living room cleaned or not is really inconsequential in comparison.

"Remember you are dust and to dust you shall return."

Remember that those things you are doing today to increase yourself are dust. As the writer of Ecclesiastes says, they are smoke.

However, and here is where life gets interesting, you do not have to be dust. You do not have to resign yourself to smoke. In Christ, through Christ, you can have love. You can be love if you will retrain your focus from yourself to Him. Do you let Him order your day, or do you insist on planning your own? Do you let Him control you, or do you seek to control Him—putting Him off until prayer time for example? Do you turn your God walkie-talkie on and listen for His messages to you, or do you do like a friend of mine who said, "I thought we just lived. I didn't know there were lessons!"

There are ultimately two things in this life: Love and Fear. Fear is an illusion, a lie of Satan. Love is real. Love is all that is real. Everything else is dust.

When the great entrepreneur J.D. Rockefeller died, a reporter asked his accountant, "How much did J.D. leave behind?" To which the accountant replied, "All of it." He left the dust of this world behind and took only the love he had for God and for others to his eternity.

As my sister said, "All we get to keep is the love we have shared with others, with God, and with ourselves."

So, I wonder how often I am dust and how often I am love. Reality is, I can be either one.

The priest on Ash Wednesday pointed this out very nicely. He said (I paraphrase), "Which is it? The Bible says not to hide your light under a bush, but then it says, 'When you do a good deed, don't let your left hand know what your right hand is doing.' It says, 'Feed my sheep,' but it also says, 'What you do in secret, your Father sees.' So which is it?"

I propose to you this points out the dust or love question nicely for the reality is, it is BOTH and it is NEITHER. Both when why you are doing it is for love. Neither if you are doing it for yourself. Pride is the first deadly sin for a reason. Pride in self and your own accomplishments will get you a handful of dust in a hurry.

When you are working from love and really letting Christ work through you in love, it matters not if your actions are public or private—they are blessed because God blesses what is Holy. If He did it, it's Holy. If you did it (even for Him), it is not. God does not bless our effort if our effort is motivated by our own self-interest (and that might even mean if we're trying to get into Heaven because of it).

For example, let's say that you decide: In order to get to Heaven, I have to read my Bible every night and visit the sick once a week. So you read your Bible every night and you visit the sick once a week. Your goal in both exercises is your own benefit—you're doing them to get to Heaven (or if you're a fear-based Christian to save yourself from Hell). The problem is this is smoke and will count for naught on the other side.

Now, let's say instead that a stranger has dropped his books all over the sidewalk. You are in a hurry to get to work, but you stop and help him because he needs help. I submit to you, that this action will survive the grave and accompany you to Heaven. You have extended love, and love lasts. Yes, it was a small thing, took no more than two minutes, but I believe it will outweigh all those other things you did in order to gain something for yourself.

Look for those moments to give love to someone else. Look for those moments when listening is all that is required. Look for those moments when Christ nudges you to help, to listen, to answer, to hear, to run, to walk, to be. Let God who ordered the whole universe order your day as well. Let love be your guiding light and realize that everything else is dust.

The more you remember you are love and to love you shall return, the more you will be living with Christ as your focus and with God in your heart. Those are the things that matter. Get that right, and everything else will follow. (2006)

No Plan B

As I write this, at least two dramatic things are happening in my life. First, a script of mine has been selected as a semi-finalist in the Kairos Prize contest. Second, I'm reading John Ortberg's *If You Want to Walk on Water, You Have to Get Out of the Boat*. What does one have to do with the other?

Well, the most frequent question I've gotten since I found out about the semi-finalist thing is: "So what now? What's next?" Upon considering this question, two things immediately pop into mind. What if I don't win? What if I do?

It took me a while to figure out that the answer to both questions is the same. "I will trust God that He has a plan, and all I must do is follow it. Whatever happens, I will simply take the next step He asks me to take whatever that next step is."

Now, I was not always like this. There was a time I spent a lot of time thinking about: "What if it doesn't work? Ugh. Then what? Should I submit it somewhere else? Should I not? Maybe it wasn't good enough and I should give up on that one. Or maybe it really is on the cusp and simply has to find the right person to read it." And then, even as those thoughts were present, so were these: "What if it wins? What will I do? Will I have to go to L.A.? I don't know if I want to do that. What if they start asking me questions that I don't know how to answer or asking me to go places I'm not ready to go? What if I have to be in the presence of actors and directors and producers? I don't think I can handle that! Maybe it would be better if I lost, at least that I've had practice at."

In all honesty the night I first found out, there were several moments in which these types of thoughts would start through my head. Thanks to some conversations with Holy Spirit friends, I have come to understand these thoughts for what they are: waves that take my focus off of Jesus. So, when I caught myself doing that in the early moments, I consciously said, "Staci, stop it. Put your eyes on Christ. He's all that matters." And instantly, my awareness of the waves ceased and all that was there was Jesus, His love for me, and His assurance that whatever happens is His will and He will be with me every step of the way.

Tonight I was reading "the boat book" (the other title's too long). In it I found this quote:

"Waiting on the Lord is the continual, daily decision to say: 'I will trust You and I will obey You. Even though the circumstances of my life are not turning out the way I want them to, and may never turn out the way I choose, I'm betting everything on You. I have no Plan B.'"

So, that's my answer to the question of "What happens next?" What happens next is I trust Him. I obey Him. I wait when He says, "Wait." I go when He says, "Go." And I go for broke that He knows what He's doing with my life whether it makes sense to me in any single moment or not.

I have no Plan B. There are no contingency plans, no alternate strategies, no back up plans. He's it. He is the Plan, and I believe in the middle of everything that I am that there really is no need for Plan B. There is need for Him and only Him. Since He is here with me, why would I ever need a Plan B?   (2007)

Power and Peace

There are many words to substitute for this lesson, so please use the words that resonate most with you. Maybe what you want to be in this life is happy, or maybe it's peaceful. What I'm talking about is that feeling that says, "Everything's okay. My world is okay, but more than that, I am okay." I am secure. I am at peace. I am happy. That's the concept we're examining.

The world—or your ego or the disempowering spiritual forces at work in the universe—will tell you that, "Yes, what you want is possible to have, but to have it, you must do *this*." Whatever *this* happens to be. What I'm realizing is the *this* is often bound up in you obtaining some external power in this world.

For example, let's say that you have come to believe that to be happy, you have to have a certain level of education. Not just an education, but the right education. You have to go to the right school, take the right classes, get the right grades, gain the right diploma—or you will never have the power to create your world in a way that will make you happy.

So you strive to gain that education because you believe it will give you the power you need in order to make your life what it will have to be to make you happy. I wish there were a softer way to say this because it may well burst the carefully constructed illusions you've built to this point. But the reality is: the right diploma will *not* give you the happiness you are seeking. In fact, when you get that diploma, you may end up asking the Anthony Robbins' question, "Is this all there is?"

The term disillusionment comes to mind.

Of course, our solution is that it must not have been the education that would do it after all. It must be the job we can get because of the education we now have. So we set our sights on that goal. And we strive and we strive, and we get the job. Okay, we should be happy now. Right?

Well, no. Actually we're still miserable. So we look at our world, and we conclude: What I really need is a promotion. Then I will have more money and more power, and then I will be happy. So we strive and we strive, and we get the promotion. Now we should be happy, but are we? No.

The problem of course is that we have the job, but we don't have the family. So we set out to get the goal of finding our "better half." It may take awhile, but finally we've found the person we were meant to spend the rest of our lives with. Pop the bubbly! Now, finally, we can be happy.

And we are… for about two minutes. Then we realize that our better half comes with baggage and issues that make our lives more stressful than we even were on our own. We're not more happy. We're less happy. So the solution, of course, is to have kids—because we all know that having kids is the ultimate in power. With our kids we can do everything differently than our parents did because we are sure that if they had just done everything right, we wouldn't feel this gnawing at our spirits that we should be happy, but we're not.

So we have kids. Now I don't know if you have kids, but let me tell you from experience—kids do *not* increase our belief in our own power, knowledge, and understanding. If anything, we quickly realize how powerless we are in the face of how to raise a child, how to make a bad day go away, how best to dry tears and build self-esteem. Good grief! We know nothing!

Of course the solution to this can be found in one of these answers:

Have another child
Get a bigger and better promotion
Make more money
Go back to work
Quit work
Get a divorce
Join community/church clubs and organizations to feel needed
Quit everything to "find ourselves"

And on and on and on.

I'm not sure if you're getting my point yet, but for those of you who haven't grasped this: NONE OF THESE WORK. None of them. If you are looking for your power to be gained from anything outside yourself, if you are looking to any of this to give your life meaning, to be the source of your acceptance, to be what will give you peace and happiness, then, my friend, you will never be happy nor at peace.

Why? Because happiness and peace do not come from anything outside. They can only come from within. Only when you tap into the True Power within you will you find contentment, peace, and happiness.

I grew up on success teaching. This teaching showed you how to have goals, to work to meet those goals, to accrue power to yourself so that you could be a "success." Of course the unspoken but inherent belief was that if you were successful, then you would get what you really want which is to be at peace and to be happy. Because the reality is, who wants success if you're just going to be miserable when you get there? "Success" seemed synonymous with "happiness" and "peace" although it really in't.

That's why we're all so confused when a millionaire kills himself. What's that phrase? "But he had so much to live for." If he had so much to live for, why did he kill himself? And the more we ponder this question, the more confused we become. For "if I was him and I had all that money and those houses and that beautiful wife, I'd be living it up! You wouldn't see me whining much less killing myself."

The truth is that we should bless these men who in their tragedy have pointed out the futility of going for what the *world* says will make us happy. They have shown us that all the cars, money, houses, marriages, divorces, kids, promotions in the world will not bring us the happiness and peace we so desire. They have shown us in black and white that the world's answers are not answers—they are traps. In fact, they are deadly traps.

So, what then? Happiness and peace are not attainable in this world? We're meant to be miserable? Pull up a chair and sit down because nothing we do can bring us what we want?

No, there is an answer, but it is not a worldly answer. It is the *only* thing that can give us True Power. True Power comes from He who is all powerful. God Almighty.

However, God's power cannot be earned nor can it be bargained for. The only way to truly attain God's power is by renouncing our own, and boy, is that tough!

I have seen the truth of this in my own life over and over again since I began to think this way and be this way in the world. A situation will happen that I *know* I cannot handle. It is simply overwhelming. It would be impossible for me to handle it, and I know it because I have had to get really honest with myself about my ability to gain power through my own resources and abilities. I have had to face the fact that of myself, I am powerless, of myself, I'm at the whims of life.

But the moment, as Marianne Williamson calls it, the Holy Instant that I can let go of me having to do anything and step back in my spirit so that God can step forward into a situation… in that moment I am most powerful.

As illogical as this sounds, the more I proclaim my powerlessness to God and ask Him to do it for me, the more powerful I appear to the world, and the more powerfully I step into situations—even those that appear completely overwhelming. I have done things that I considered completely impossible, and they would've been for me on my own. But I know I'm not the one doing them. When these things happen, when life just works out because I relied on Him, I *get it* on a very deep level that I never have to be afraid. I can have peace and happiness and hope at any moment I so choose simply by relinquishing my control and my power in the situation to His.

St. Paul understood that "in my weakness, Your strength is illuminated, and so I boast in my weakness." This concept is completely illogical to our human way of thinking, and yet, I will tell you from experience that it's true.

You don't have to do it—whatever "it" is. You can't. When you get that, when you take the leap of faith to believe that, you can then ask for Real Power to begin to operate in your life. You will stop chasing the rainbows that the world holds out to be "the answer." You will never again get to a place and think, "Is this all there is?" because you realize that all there ever is, is right now. This moment is all you will ever have if you cling to the illusion that you have the power to cause life to be anyway other than it is right now. And this moment is all there ever is if you proclaim your powerlessness and let Him take over.

It may well take painful disillusionment to get you to see that any power you're relying on other than God is an illusion. It may require that your "kingdoms fall" for you to see that you don't have the power. You never have, and you never will. This is not fatalistic. It's realistic. Moreover, it is ultimately empowering to a degree that I cannot adequately explain.

You can either learn this truth through going through your own painful disillusionments, or you can take my word for it, learn from my experience, and begin your journey to True Power, peace, and happiness at this very moment. How? By getting quiet with yourself and saying,

"Lord, I'm beginning to see now that all my efforts to make my world be how I thought it had to be so that I could be happy and at peace have really only shown me how miserable I really am. I see that now, so Lord, as scary as it is, I am willing to relinquish my attempts to gain power of my own ability. I am willing to stop putting my faith in the external 'things of this world'—money, education, work, my spouse, my children, my community, my service—and expecting them to bring me joy. I realize that those things cannot give me peace and joy because only You can give peace and joy. I commit myself now to the Holy Instant when I can remember that You are the true source of power, and I can call on You at any moment I feel powerless, and Your Power will step in. Please remind me so that in those moments when I most need You I will not be tempted to go on my own strength. I am willing to practice being powerless in the full faith that in my powerlessness, Your power will so take over the situation (and my entire life) that miracles will happen before my eyes. I thank You and I praise You for showing me this lesson in concrete terms. May this Holy Instant be the start of my brand new life—the life You had envisioned for me from the very beginning of time. Amen." (2006)

The Butterfly Effect

I really wish I had taken physics. It seems to me the more in-tuned people I listen to, the more they refer to laws of physics. That's logical I guess seeing how I mostly read and listen to those who speak about God and His infinite wisdom. Of course the God who positioned the earth on an axis where one degree off would've meant no atmosphere—and by extension no human race—probably put the rest of our laws together that brilliantly as well.

So it was with great interest that I listened to Andy Andrews, the author of several amazing books, speak about the Butterfly Effect. According to Mr. Andrews, the Butterfly Effect is in essence that a butterfly on one side of the world flaps its wings, moving molecules, which push into other molecules and those in turn push other molecules getting bigger and bigger until it can create a hurricane on the other side of the world.

He then goes on to explain this principle as it relates to our lives. He takes the story of Norman Borlog, a winner of the Nobel Peace Prize who figured out how to use a hybrid of corn and wheat that literally saved the lives of two billion people—so far. But Mr. Andrews says, it wasn't really Mr. Borlog who saved all those lives because many years before, a man by the name of Henry Wallace hired Mr. Borlog to work in a station in Mexico whose mission it was to find a way to hybridize corn and wheat.

So obviously it was Mr. Wallace who saved those two billion people. Or was it? Mr. Andrews continues that many years prior to Mr. Wallace hiring Mr. Borlog, Mr. Wallace was known only as Henry—a little six year old kid. And when he was a six year old kid, Henry came into contact with George Washington Carver, who took this little boy under his wing and taught him about agriculture. So it makes sense that it was Mr. Washington Carver who saved the two billion people, right? Or was it Moses Carver?

Moses Carver? Who's that? And what did he have to do with any of this? Well, Mr. Andrews continues that Moses Carver through an act of sheer will and sacrifice on his own part saved the life of a baby who then was adopted into Moses Carver's own family. That baby was... you guessed it... George Washington Carver.

I'm sure if we could go back, again there would be someone who taught Moses Carver about sacrifice and making decisions that matter, and there would be someone behind that person, and someone behind that person. And on and on and on.

Historically this is fascinating, but think what it means futuristically. Are you the kind of person who thinks to take a six year old kid under your wing, teach them, mentor them, and change the course of the world forever? Are you the kind of person who makes sacrifices, who uses your time and talent to better the world, or are you just trying to get through the day? Do you make decisions that affect your tomorrow? Of course you do, but what kind of decisions are you making, and would you make different ones if you really believed the butterfly effect was real?

The butterfly effect is real. I have seen it work in person. I have seen something I did and believed to be just a simple act change the course of someone's life. Then I have witnessed that person make a simple act that changed the course of someone else's life. I have seen friends who used things we've talked about to teach kids about God. I have seen those kids who learned about God, turn and be a force for positive change in our world. It's the Butterfly Effect in action!

I believe after hearing about the Butterfly Effect, that harnessed by enough of the right "butterflies" (and just so you know, that's anyone who's willing to do it), we could change our world by being willing to beat our wings to help others in our world. If you are interested in experimenting for yourself, I challenge you... Today, find a way—small or large—to beat your butterfly wings. But don't stop today. Do it again tomorrow, and the next day, and the next, and somewhere down the line we could have a hurricane of kindness, goodness, generosity, and hope sweep across this great land of ours and retake the world.

From where I'm sitting, this is one law of physics that would be worth learning! (2006)

The Ultimate Identity Crisis

Who are you? No. Really. Stop for a moment, and answer that question. If I say, "Tell me about yourself. Who are you?" What would you tell me?

I'm sure some would say, "Well, I'm a mom (or a dad)... I'm a wife (or a husband)... I'm single... I'm divorced... I'm a banker, or a lawyer, or a housewife... I'm an accountant, or a teacher, or a TV salesman..."

Okay, that's all well and good, but I want something deeper than who the world sees. I want to know who you are, not what your label or the box society has put you in says. Who are you?

Drop down into those characteristics that make up your character, your identity. "I'm an honest man who does his best to live as a Christian... I'm someone who loves people and who does my best to serve..." Or maybe your answer would be something like this, "I'm my own worst enemy... I'm someone who no matter how hard I try, I can't seem to get things right..."

These are the realms of consciousness and sometimes unconsciousness that we're talking about. About who you really are, or about who you think you really are. I encourage you to take a moment to jot down five of these character type statements about who you are (and be honest. No one else will ever see nor read these.) Got your five?

If not, do it.

Got it? Okay. Now let's talk.

You may think after writing these down that now's a bad time to mention this, but did you put anything in your short identity statements about your identity in Christ? Did you mention who you are in God's eyes? Did you even give any thought to the identity He's already given you?

For we have put on Christ…

Our reality is that whatever we sincerely believe about ourselves is who we manifest to the world. We all know of stories of kids who came from the same home—one went on to help the world, the other went to jail. Why? Simply, the end is present in the moment by moment regard each held about themselves. If you believe you are worthless, then your actions will reflect that. If you believe you are destined for greatness, your actions will reflect that.

Others in the world—parents, teachers, friends, family—they all shape and mold who we think we are, but the truth is that once we get to be adults, we are the ones who choose what to believe about ourselves. We can choose, and sometimes (often times) we choose very poorly.

One of the ways we choose poorly is by listening to Satan when he starts playing his little, evil, insidious tricks. Let's say for example that there is a woman who in her heart of hearts feels she is empty. She is scared and struggling, but to the whole world she looks like the model of a perfect Christian. She is at church every week, sometimes two or three times. She is in the Ladies Society and the choir. Her kids are always dressed to the nines, and her house is meticulously kept.

However well all the outside accoutrements mask her true evaluation of herself to the outside world, they do not cover her evaluation when she looks at herself. She never feels good enough. If her son pitches a fit at church, she knows everyone is looking at her and judging her an incompetent mother. If her marriage hits a rough patch, she avoids getting help because of "how would it look."

The reality is that her life and her energy are wrapped in the increasingly desperate pursuit of two things: First, keeping up the appearance that everything is all right, and second, filling the emptiness she feels with anything that might make her feel less lonely, less trapped, less frightened, less lost, less powerless.

So what does she try to fill it with? Could be many things, and some look like very positive behavior… work, involvement with her kids, her kids' pursuits and accomplishments, the things she can buy, the parties she can go to, the money she (and her husband) make, her house, her involvement in church and community activities and organizations.

In essence these things slowly become her identity. They twine together until even she believes to a large extent that they are her. There are moments in which she sees that her true self is empty. She feels it when she stops long enough to notice, so her solution is not to stop, not to notice.

What we have here is the real definition of an identity crisis. Satan has convinced her that her identity is all these outside things. Have you ever heard of identity theft?

This is a good definition of it. Satan has convinced her that her identity is not what it truly is, and placing your identity on the shifting sands of what's out there is a sure way of feeling empty and trapped and terrified. If you feel this is where your life is or is headed, the solution is to take back your identity immediately. But how do you do that?

The answer lies in one word. God. The answer is to go to God—not to the outside world—to find your true identity. Your true identity is that you are marvelously and wonderfully made. Your true identity is that you have been bought and paid for by the Blood of Jesus Christ. Your true identity is that God poured out His love in making you, and then did it again in saving you, and then did it again by leading you to articles just like this one.

Your identity is set in His assessment of you, and His assessment of you has nothing to do with you. I know. Huh? The truth of the matter is that the old saying, "God doesn't make junk" has more to do with God than with the junk. God loves you not because of anything you've done or not done. He loves you because God is love. That's what He does, and that is not shifting sand. That is a Rock that stands in good times and bad times, regardless of what the world says.

Your worth is not grounded in if you make every decision right. It is not grounded in if you have made every decision right thus far. Even though you haven't, He loves you because He is God, and God is love. So how about answering "Who are you?" by saying, "I am a child of the Most High King who loves me more than I will ever, ever know."

Ground your identity in *that* understanding, and you will never again be in jeopardy of being a victim of Satan's identity theft nor even a more common identity crisis because your identity will be set on the Rock. That's a great place to start. (2006)

Like Carrie

Carrie is a good person. I want that stated first lest you think I am somehow running her down. Carrie has a prayer life that in part consists of getting up early in the morning and spending time with God. She reads. She prays. She meditates.

One morning at a prayer group she shared her experience with us, and it truly was awesome. A friend of mine in the group decided to adopt Carrie's approach to prayer.

Betty, my friend, was pumped. She was ready to pray like Carrie. The first morning all went very well. The second it was good. By the third Betty noticed that instead of being in the Word, she was more asleep than awake. "I kept waking up going, 'What'd that say?'" By the fourth morning she was angry with herself. Guilt and self-judgment conspired to throw her confidence in the plan down a sink hole.

She said, "I just kept thinking, 'Carrie can do this. Why can't I?'"

The answer may be as obvious to you as it was to me; however, I challenge you right now to look at your life and see where you are doing the same thing. Where are you bashing yourself because you can't do it just like so-and-so?

Of course the reason you can't do it like that person is because you are not that person! You are you, and knowing that, you have to take the desire in your heart and find what works for you.

I know many writers who plot an entire book from the first page to the last. They know every plot point and surprise before they ever put a word on paper. And the truth is, that works for them. But another truth is that it doesn't work for me. It drives me crazy.

If I can see the whole book before I write, what's the point of writing? For me, I have to write and let the plot points fall where they may. Neither approach is good or bad, right or wrong. They are just different.

One morning Betty got up and got real. "This isn't working. I have to find a way to make it work for me." That's when she let go of being Carrie and started being Betty.

Instead of getting up and starting prayer time immediately, she began getting ready for work first and then having prayer time. She said, "When I do that, I'm more awake, and I get so much more out of it."

The really awesome part of all of this is God doesn't require us all to do it like Carrie. We can be Carrie and Betty and Staci... And it is as it was meant to be.

Let go of being someone else. Be you. That's all God asks. (2006)

Lifting Your Hands

It's sad how difficult we make being a Christian. We do it to ourselves and to each other—putting rules and conditions on ourselves once we're saved. Before we're saved, we're told, "You can't do it. Jesus is your salvation." After we're saved, we're told, "Okay, here's the rules. You can do this. You can't do that. Don't even think about doing that." And I'm not even talking about the big rules like killing someone or being envious of their position. I'm talking about pickiness that goes way beyond that.

For example, in my line of work—Christian romance writing, there are "rules," some call them "standards." They go like this:

You can't have anyone in your story drink alcohol because some of our readers don't believe in drinking.

You can't have anyone in your story dance. Ditto number one.

No sitting on laps. That's too intimate.

No taking off clothes—even if the character is alone and it's completely innocent.

No showers.

Do not show the character in bed even alone. And the character may never be described as being in their pajamas—even if they are alone because that is suggestive.

Now, I'm sure they have their reasons for all these rules, but for me, rules are not where it's at. We spent thousands of years with the Old Testament going around and around and around that mountain to come to the conclusion that rules don't work! We can't do it. Only God can.

Personally, I think we are far more like a baby who is trying to walk than a god who can come up with enough rules to keep ourselves in line. Further, I think we can learn a lot about how God loves us by watching a good parent with a baby.

A child who is learning to walk first stands, and when he falls, a good parent does not huff in disgust at the child's "failure." A good parent does not condemn the child, call him worthless, and give up on him. No. A good parent immediately picks the child up, praises him, loves him, and encourages him to try again.

Now does the parent pretty much know the child will fall again? Sure. If you've ever been there when a child takes his first steps, you know they are going to fall. Does that deter the good parent from praising and applauding each and every small step the child takes? No. Because they know it's their praise that will encourage the child to take another.

This is just as it is with our Heavenly Father. He is ecstatic when we take a step—even a faltering one—toward Him. From my own experience with my kids, it wouldn't surprise me if God called all the angels in to watch. "Oh, look! Johnny took another step toward real understanding of Me, toward really learning to be loving!" And, I'm equally sure that the angels for love of the child's Father if nothing else get excited as well.

Does God know we will fall again? Sure. Does that deter Him from getting excited about each positive step we take? No. He, like any good parent, is right there cheering us on, encouraging, praising, smiling at the steps we are taking.

I think the most applause comes when we take not worldly accomplishment steps, but Heavenly accomplishment steps. When we learn to have a little more faith, when we learn to be a little more loving, when we learn to be compassionate and have mercy. I just know God is up there, tears in His eyes for how proud He is of us. I know because I've sat on the floor as my children took their first steps to me, and there is simply no other reaction than tears of joy.

In fact, we would all be much better off if we spent our time as little children, our arms up-reaching to let God pick us up than concocting rules to get ourselves "good enough" to spend eternity with Him. The truth is, we are babies in need of a Heavenly Father who loves us show much, He is willing to be patient when we fall because He knows (better than we do) that falling is part of the learning process.

It would be wise for us all to remember that about each other as well. Then we might hear the applause of Heaven because we have taken another small step toward becoming the loving child of God He meant us to be. (2006)

Just Hanging Out

Have you ever tried to be a Christian so hard it hurts? Have you ever done all the right things and still felt like you were completely missing something? I think at some point or another we've all been there—reading the Bible, going to church, serving, doing, doing, doing all the right things, but it's so hard. It's hard to get motivated to read the Bible. It's hard to get motivated to teach that Sunday school class or to even go to church.

Would it surprise you to find out you're not alone in having felt that? I'm guessing it would surprise you. I know it would've surprised me a few years ago to find I wasn't the only one "dutying myself" to a spiritual death. But, boy, did I look good doing it!

I knew all the prayers, could recite them at blazing speed, which I did to get through them. I went to church, volunteered, served, joined, read, but to be honest, there were at best flashes of joy. Every so often I would get a glimpse of how cool it is to be with God, but mostly it was just work.

This morning a friend emailed. She related a story that made me laugh out loud because it encapsulates the shift that my life and my relationship with God has gone through in the past three years.

Here it is in her words: "Adoration was awesome today. The guy that snores was there so it was hard to concentrate. But God really spoke to me, I was reading my Bible but not absorbing what I was reading, I heard God say, 'Hey, put it down, and just hang out with me.' So I was still and the snoring stopped. It was then I heard how much I am loved!!!! AIN'T GOD GREAT?!"

Doesn't that make your spirit smile? It sure did mine.

I have come to the conclusion that we spend so much time trying to do all the right things that we miss the point of doing them in the first place. The point of reading the Bible and going to church is simply to have some time to hang out with God. Once you get that, you will see that's all He really wants to do anyway.

He's not interested in heartless obedience. He made you for a reason, and the reason is so that He would have someone to love. Think of it this way, God is standing right next to you as you sit to read the Bible. You have a goal to read one chapter because that will prove how much you love Him, plus it will meet some requirement you're sure is written on some requirement book in Heaven.

So you sit down to read. As you start, God says, "Hi, I'm so glad you came." Immediately, you get annoyed and anchor your attention more forcefully to the page. After a moment God tries again, "Did you notice that sunset out there? It is a real work of art." Of course, you don't hear the whole thing. You just looked up and noticed the sunset. "UGH! This reading the Bible is so difficult. I can't keep my mind on what it's saying." In fact, that must be why He requires it, to test just how serious we are in our commitment. Right?

For fifteen, twenty, thirty minutes we diligently push all other thoughts out of our head. Then we read that magic last word. Like a prisoner released, we spring from the chair. Free to go on about our life—duty finished. Of course we feel no more filled with God's love than we did when we sat down. Why? Because God's still standing there, wishing we would stop trying to impress Him and learn to just hang out with Him.

Since I've gotten off the performance treadmill and started just hanging out with Him, life has gotten so cool! Let me tell you, He's an awesome friend. We laugh together, cry together, plan together, live together.

Do I read the Bible? You bet I do! Who wouldn't want to hang out with their best friend? But when I do, I also tune in to what He is telling me. And sometimes all He wants me to do is what Mary did—just sit at His feet, gaze to Him, and listen. Just be with Him. Just hang out.

Martha, Martha, you are worried and bothered about many things; but only a few things are necessary, really only one, for Mary has chosen the good part, which shall not be taken from her. – Luke 10:41-42

The time you spend just hanging out with Christ will never be taken from you because it is the only thing necessary. Try it sometime. I bet you'll be pleasantly surprised how full of His love you are when you get up.

Just hanging out with God is cool. (2006)

Jesus Wept

I have always had interpretations of the Bible verse, "Jesus wept." It happened in the Garden of Gethsemane when Jesus was talking with God about the upcoming trial and crucifixion. Also in this scene is the famous line, "Father, if … this cup…" In my mind I had always put the two together and figured Jesus was probably weeping because He was afraid of going through what He was facing.

Another interpretation I have surmised is that Jesus was looking all the way down through the centuries to me, to my sins that would nail Him to a tree and bleed Him dry until He loved me to death. I thought that maybe He was weeping for all the hurt my sins had caused, all the pain He saw as He looked down through the ages and saw what horrible things we do to each other sometimes even in the name of God.

I still think these two interpretations may be valid. It may be a case of all of the above. However, in the last couple of weeks, I have found yet another interpretation that I think also fits. The short version of the story is this: A friend of mine and I had a fight. Now it wasn't much of a fight exactly because I still don't know what I did to upset her, but it's pretty clear after three weeks of not talking to me that she is upset.

One evening we happened to be at church at the same time. When it came time for the sign of peace, I went over to her to shake her hand. We hugged, and then knowing I had to, I stepped away and went back to my bench. I couldn't help but cry. Interestingly, I wasn't crying because she doesn't love me. First, I know she does. Second, it didn't really matter because I'm okay. I know it will work out the way it is meant to. I know God still loves me and nothing that happens here can take that away.

The reason I was crying was because she wouldn't let me love her. She was obviously hurting. She obviously needed someone, and yet as good of friends as we are, she won't let me help her. At that second, I got it. Jesus was looking at us all through the centuries, and He didn't cry because we didn't love Him. No, He was crying because of the times we wouldn't let Him love us. Believe me, I know now how much that hurts.

Whatever you're going through today, good or bad, let Him love you. That's all He wants. (2006)

I Want Them to Say…

The other night I got to talk extensively with one of my favorite Holy Spirit friends—my sister. Since we both have families to keep up with now, that doesn't happen as often as it used to, so we really took advantage of this time. Late into the night we talked about what God is doing in our lives and about how He has recently been bringing up places in each of us that need to be healed.

As we talked, she said, "You know, ever since I was first married, I had one goal. I wanted to be the best mom to my kids. I wanted them to say when they were grown up, 'We had the best Mom. She was so great.'" On the whole not a bad dream. I think many of us moms think exactly the same thing.

However, she didn't stop there. She said, "Now I see how that dream is about me. It's about what I want to hear because I want to have earned that. Then they other day, I realized that I don't care if they ever say that about me. What I want them to say more than anything is: 'We have the best God ever! He is so great!' Now I think if they say that when they get older, I will have done my job."

Wow. I was blown away. Not just for her, but for me.

You see, the business of writing often starts as a desire just to write. You just love to write, and so you do. Then you get a little better and a little better, and pretty soon, you begin to sense that "just writing" is not enough. Now, you want to be published. So, you begin to learn the rules of publishing, and you work, and you hone, and you learn. And pretty soon, a new goal creeps into your soul. "I want to touch a lot of people with my words about God. I want not just to be published, but to be thought of by many as a great writer."

After our conversation, I see that for what it is… having your focus on the WRONG GOAL. It's like my eighth grade girls' basketball team. It was our second game of the year. The first half went by, we went to the locker room, came back out, and were ready to start the second half. Now if you don't know, when you start the second half, the teams switch ends of the court.

They tipped off. Our girl got it and proceed to dribble to the other team's goal where she made the shot! Her technique was great, her shot flawless, but the problem was, she was shooting at the wrong goal!

I wonder how many of us want to be the best... the best fathers, mothers, sisters, brothers, friends, writers, accountants, salespeople, workers... And yet, we are shooting at the wrong goal.

In the last 24-hours my life goal has changed. I no longer want everyone to think I'm the best writer. If somehow, they see through my writing that He is the best God ever, and their lives begin to reflect that, then I have accomplished the new goal for my life.

How about you? Are you shooting at the wrong goal—wanting to be the best salesperson, counselor, or teacher? Maybe God is asking that you start being those things in a way that points people to the best God ever. You do that, and whatever else you do, you will be successful. (2005)

He Doesn't Care About the Cupcakes

I remember that day so very well. I was young – four or five. We did something unusual that day, unusual for my house at least. We made cupcakes. With my mom helping out on our family owned and operated dairy, there wasn't much time for cupcake-baking. But that day, for whatever reason, we made cupcakes.

At that point in time my grandfather, who later lost his sight to diabetes, could still see. Also at that time he had several horses only a quarter-mile from our house. That day my grandpa happened to be out with the horses, and one of us, my mom or me, decided that I should take him a cupcake.

Now from the time I was small, missions were very important to me. I held my responsibilities in very high regard. I didn't want to simply do things – I wanted to do them perfectly. So I set out, barefoot, from my house, cupcake in hand, bound for the pen where my grandpa was working.

However, when I got there, I found a huge problem for a little girl with a cupcake in her hand – the fence that separated me from Grandpa's side. There was a gate connecting the fence. It was an old gray aluminum number with about four horizontal slots held together with one long diagonal slot. At five or so feet tall, it was a monster.

Worse, whatever held it upright didn't hold it steady. So the gate swayed dangerously top down with any pressure applied to it. For little me, that gate presented a big problem. I wasn't big enough to open it. I couldn't yell loud enough for Grandpa to hear me. So as I surveyed the situation in my little mind, I decided my only option was to climb the thing.

I only hope that now I would be smart enough to set the cupcake through the gate before I started climbing. Unfortunately, I didn't think that far ahead that day. Instead, cupcake in hand, I started climbing.

The journey was going pretty well until I got to the top. As I hiked my first let over the top slot, I ran out of hands to keep me stable just as the gate swayed the other direction. I remember Grandpa yelling for me to stop and wait. I remember saying something like, "Grandpa, look! I brought you a cupcake."

The next thing I remember is hitting the hard ground on the other side with a body-whacking thud. And then I remember seeing the cupcake smashed to a flat, chocolate mud pie next to me. Grandpa made it to me about ten seconds after I hit the ground. I was absolutely hysterical. He picked me up and held me, telling me it would be okay and asking if I was hurt.

All I could think was I had smashed the cupcake. His cupcake. I had failed the mission. I had let him down.

It took me many long years to learn the lesson of that day. The truth was: He didn't care about the stupid cupcake. He cared about me.

I learned this only when I realized that is exactly how God is with us. We're all worried about the cupcakes we've made and are bringing to Him – like our accomplishments and our good deeds and our ministries. But the reality is He doesn't care about our cupcakes – He cares about us! And it really doesn't matter to Him if our cupcakes get smashed along the way or if they were ever perfect in the first place. All He cares about is being able to hold us so He can ask what's wrong, where are we hurt, and being able to hold us until we're all better.

It took me a long time to be grateful for falling over that gate, but now that I see the lesson, those cupcakes, those missions, and being perfect don't seem nearly as important. What's important, all that's important, is He loves me. Everything else is cupcakes, and He doesn't care about the cupcakes. (2005)

Falling In Love With Him

For many years of my life I thought I understood how God wanted to be with us. He was the Master; we were His servants. He gave the orders; we followed His commands. It was a King to servant type of relationship.

I tried to be a good servant. I really did. I sang in choirs, was a member of the CYO. I was an usher, a reader, and I even headed a during-church nursery. I was a good servant.

Sometime ago I began to feel a change in myself as to how I was relating to Christ. Although it's difficult to explain, I can easily see how different this new relationship is.

I think it could be analogous to falling in love. There is the first meeting—the one that takes you off-guard. What is this? This is new. I've never felt this way before. This is at the beginning.

Then comes the dating phase of falling in love. This phase is first characterized with effort to impress the other. Overwhelmed with the accompanying feelings of love of someone else, we want at all costs to keep them liking us. That's where I was—trying to make Christ like me. I felt like He did (most of the time anyway), but I wasn't totally sure why. After all, if He knew the real me, why would He want to stay around? If He knew the real me, He would know about the times I was less than perfect, and let's face it, who wants to be with someone who's less than perfect?

But then there came a time—not one moment, but a whole bunch of little ones strung together. Little by little, I began to let go of having to be perfect when I went to Him. Just as those who are falling in love do, I began to let Him see me not only when I was in control, but also when I wasn't. I began to go to Him when I was confused and afraid. When things didn't go my way and I needed a shoulder to cry on, I went to Christ, and He was there every single time.

This was not the relationship of a Master to a servant. It was something truly new.

As I let go, our time together became less about Him giving commands and more about just being together. Instead of reading His Word out of duty, I began to read it just to get closer to Someone I was falling in love with.

In a relationship there comes a time when all you want to do is be with the other person. You think about them constantly, and when you're away from them, you long to get close again.

That's where I am now. I want to be with Christ. I want to know Him, to see where He is in my life, to love Him not because I have to but because I want to.

I now see that the Master/servant relationship was a mere shell in comparison to the relationship we now share. In a very real sense I am falling in love with Jesus. And it's the best thing that's ever happened to me. (2006)

Ever Faithful

For many years of my life, I wanted to be successful. I put a lot of effort into that endeavor. I worked and worked and worked. If I joined an organization, I had to be president because I wanted the organization to be successful and I wanted to be seen as a success in the organization. Success was my goal.

After I started writing, I turned my success-orientation toward God. I wanted to be a success for Him. Somehow I thought that would prove to Him I was worthy of His love and gain me a place in His kingdom. I wanted Him to love me, and I thought the only way He would love me was if I was a success. Sad how some of us get so mixed up like that.

It took seven years of writing, three years of publishing, and a gentle but very firm re-direct from God for me to see how wrong I had been the whole time. As always, I had been working and working and working, trying to get the publishing and marketing to work out. I put an enormous amount of time and effort into that endeavor. Still, things were not pointing toward me being a success. Even when I had successes, they were too small for me to acknowledge, and so I called them failures and resolved to do better.

When I finally woke up to see that what I was doing was not what God required of me—that He didn't require me to be a success for Him to love me—that was truly a revelation. In a very real way He saved me from me!

Since then, lesson-by-lesson, I have learned to let go of doing it myself and to let Him take over the controls of my life. Not always easy for a control-freak, but by far the easier way to live once you get the hang of it.

The other night in a sermon, God spoke to me in a way that made me smile. The priest said, "God doesn't require you to be a success. He only requires that you be faithful." Well, that's about as direct a message as you could get.

However, would I have heard those words ten years ago? Probably not, but they sure resonated with me the other night.

The amazing thing is that a friend of mine and I have been talking about this very thing—being faithful. She said, "What I am learning is that God doesn't even require us to be faithful because our faithfulness is imperfect. God simply wants to show us His faithfulness."

Wow! Not only do I not have to be a success to gain God's approval, I don't even have to be perfectly faithful to gain God's approval! The more I thought about this, the clearer it became. Over and over and over again, God has shown me, "Staci, even when you fall, even when you're discouraged, even when you feel like a failure, even when you're scared, I am here—loving you, cheering you on, giving you Me."

With that understanding, how then, I ask you, could I ever feel like a failure? How could I ever think I was anything less than a success? And it has nothing at all to do with me. It has nothing to do with my performance, my plans, my control, my abilities, my knowledge, my understanding. It's all about Him.

His performance, His plans, His control, His abilities. His knowledge, His understanding, His wisdom, His love, His mercy. His faithfulness.

In a very real way, all He asks of me is that I take a step back from me, look to Him, and marvel at His faithfulness. He is ever faithful to me. Not sometimes faithful. Not faithful when it's easy or convenient. He is EVER faithful!

Just as He is ever loving. He is. And if I let my worth be based not on me but on Him, then I'm already a success.

Isn't He the coolest? (2006)

Daily Bread

"Give us this day our daily bread…"

Ask a group of Christians what this line in the Our Father means, and you will probably get something close to the following answers. Eucharist. The last supper. Food.

All possible and likely. However, here's my interpretation of "Give us this day our daily bread." Bread is life at its most basic. You eat you live. You don't, you die. Pretty simple. But it doesn't say, "Give us this day a sushi appetizer, a five-course meal, a chocolate mousse dessert, and a midnight snack to top it off." No, it says our "daily bread." The basics. Not lobster and cavier. Bread.

However, this doesn't necessarily mean bread in a literal sense. To me, it also means "the things that we really need." In fact, often when I pray the Our Father, one side of my brain is praying the prayer, the other side is interpreting it using everyday language. When I hit this line, my mouth says, "Give us this day our daily bread," but my mind and heart say, "Give me today the things I really need."

The things I *really need*. Not the things I want. Not the things it would be nice to have. Not even in an object kind of way. The "things" I really need today might be a friend's shoulder to cry on or a talk with a friend that illuminates a new layer of truth. It might be time with my kids or a safe trip home for my husband. It might be a passage of reading that is the piece I needed to fit into something I'm writing. It could be a song on the radio, a piece of a movie, a moment that changes everything. It might be a new idea for writing or an email from a friend with encouragement at just the right moment.

The best thing about praying like this is that it opens the door for God to decide what it is you most need, rather than you having to run around trying to find it. He, Who can see into eternities in the future, can make the decision that right now, this day, what you most need is... This. What an awesome way to pray.

Yes, what I really need often changes, but more than once I have noticed how what I really need suddenly shows up. I think He's always sending what we really need, and I also think the more consciously we ask for what we really need, the more He sends it into our lives. So, consider revising your interpretation of this line or at least adding a new layer of understanding to those you already have. Then watch what happens because it may suddenly become obvious that you're getting what you really need. (2005)

Being Eli

In the book of Samuel we hear the story of the call of Samuel. The boy is asleep in the temple with the Holy of Holies while Eli, Samuel's mentor is asleep elsewhere. When I was young, I always pictured myself as Samuel and wondered would I hear God if He called me. Recently I heard this story again, only this time I heard it quite differently.

You see, I believe I have heard my call except it was more of a guiding hand directing my steps that brought me where God wants me to be. There wasn't a moment that God said, "Staci, this is what I want you to do." But I feel very sure that this is what God wants me to do at least for this time.

When I heard this story again, I realized there is another person in the story—Eli, the old mentor. He is asleep, which can mean literally. It can also mean spiritually. Often we "fall asleep" in our walk with the Lord. Other things in life push in, and time to sit and just be gets crowded out. Then here comes this kid, this child whom Eli is supposed to be watching out for, and he says, "Yes, sir. Here I am. You called."

Eli is immediately puzzled. "I didn't call you. Go back to sleep."

We say this to each other and to our kids. "You don't have to go to church. If you have a game to play or something else to do, it's no big deal. Go back to sleep." As we walk through this life with others around us, very often we not only miss our own calls, we also misinterpret another's call.

For example, the wife in a married couple feels a calling to donate items to the poor. The husband questions the wife's actions because the items could at least be sold at a garage sale and bring in money for the family. Or the husband decides to make a concerted effort to go to church, but the wife drags her feet to the point that the husband gives up and stays home.

There are a thousand ways the world around us says, "No. Don't worry. Just go back to sleep."

Samuel does as instructed. He goes back to sleep; however, God is persistent. He calls the youth again. "Samuel... Samuel..."

Again, Samuel gets up and goes to Eli. "You called?"

Now Eli is frustrated. "I did not call you. Go back to sleep!"

Very often our attempts to get closer to God are met with serious resistance by the world. People get uncomfortable talking about faith, so we push ours over in the corner and determine to keep it to ourselves. After all, we don't want others to think we've lost our minds. Make no mistake, the darkness does not like the light, for where there is light the darkness necessarily vanishes. It is no different with the dark powers in the spiritual realm. When that call comes from God, they will do everything they can to convince you it's nothing. "Go back to sleep."

The third time Samuel is sleeping, and God calls, "Samuel. Samuel."

I'm sure Samuel thought he was losing his mind. I'm sure he even questioned his sanity to go wake Eli up again. But he saw no other option. After all, Eli was his master. "Yes, you called?"

Finally, finally Eli gets it. "Oh, wait. I get it. I think it's God Who's calling you..."

To me, being Samuel is tough enough. There's that whole putting yourself out there to look like an idiot to your friend and mentor. There's also the small matter of being honest about where you are in life and what's really happening.

But how many times are we Eli, and we completely mess our role up? How many times does someone come to us with a problem and instead of pointing them to the One who can help, we give them worldly answers that cause more problems than they solve? How many times do we fail to listen to God talking to us, helping us guide them to Him? How many times are we so asleep to our own walk with God that we miss the chance to give Him to someone else?

I don't know about you, but I've been Eli more times than I want to count. I just hope the next time Samuel comes to me with something God is calling him to, I will recognize what's happening the first time and point Him to the One Who lays out the plan not only for the stars and the universe but for our lives as well. (2006)

Being a Magi

A long time ago I read a book that said, "There is a reason you notice the things you notice. They come into your sight to tell you something." (paraphrase) I took that to heart and began actively noticing. That is, I notice when I notice something. Rather than going through life oblivious to the signs God is putting in my path, I either actively seek them or at least I get it with only a couple of occurrences.

This is much like the man in the flood who was standing on his porch as a boat went by. The people in the boat told him he could come with them. He shook his head. "God will save me if He wants to save me." Several hours past, and now he was hanging onto an upstairs window. A second boat came by. The people in it said, "Come on with us!" But the man replied, "No, I love God, and if He wants to save me, He will."

Hours past, and it grew dark. A Coast Guard boat with a search light found the man clinging to his chimney. "Come on! Get on!" they yelled. But the man refused. "I love God, and if He wants to save me, He will." An hour later the man appeared at the Pearly Gates.

St. Peter looked at him incredulously. "What are you doing here?" The man shrugged. "I guess it was my time. God didn't save me." To which St. Peter said, "That's weird. We sent three boats!"

After I heard this story, I once heard Oprah Winfrey say something similar. She said (paraphrase), "To get your attention, God will send a breath. Then He will send a pebble, then a brick, then a boulder, then the whole house will come crashing down!"

Let me just say, for myself, I prefer to catch what God's telling me at the first boat, the breath, or at most the pebble. So, I am very conscious of the messages God sends to me. And they are everywhere!

In music, books, the Bible, conversations, on billboards, in magazines, sometimes even in dreams. Recently I've been preparing a project that is very close to my heart for which God has given many signs and messages since it was first conceived. For this one project I have received messages ranging from videos depicting the story, songs, email messages, and even a tour bus following me down the road!

The ultimate (so far) message was that just before I mailed the project in, I was praying over it in the Post Office, and my oldest daughter said, "Look, Mom." When I opened my eyes, she was holding a piece of paper about five inches from me in my direct line of sight. It said, "Your talents will be recognized and suitably rewarded." I just started laughing because I get signs and messages, but most of the time they take at least a little bit of interpretation.

As I was recounting these events to my sister, she laughed. "You are such a Magi." To which I said the only logical thing I could think of, "Huh?"

She went on to explain. "The Magi were astronomers. They spent their time looking for signs in the sky, signs of a new king, signs of a shift on the earth begun in the heavens. That's what you do!"

I'd never thought of it quite like that, but I've got to say, it's great fun to be a Magi. You should try it sometime. (2006)

Bearing Fruit

I am the true vine, and My Father is the vinedresser. Every branch in Me that does not bear fruit, He takes away; and every branch that bears fruit, He prunes it, that it may bear more fruit. –John 15: 1-2

Every so often a different interpretation of something I thought I knew my whole life sends shock waves through my life. Thus it was with this Bible verse. I had always defined "bear" as meaning *to produce*. In other words, "Every branch in Me that does not *produce* fruit, He takes away..." Then I began reading about how God doesn't expect us to do things for Him. No, He wants to do things through us if we allow Christ and the Holy Spirit to take over our lives to such a degree that it is *them* doing the doing and not us.

Okay, but there was still this verse. Clearly it says if I am in Him, I will produce fruit. Right? Well, maybe.

I give you this new insight to ponder, not so that you can accept it outright, but so that you can try it on in your life and see if it fits.

There is a second definition of "bear" I had never considered. It is actually the first definition of the word. Bear means to carry or to hold.

Does that make any difference in how you read this verse? "Every branch in Me that does not *hold* fruit, He takes away..." To me, holding is much different than producing. Holding is passive. Someone else has done all the hard work to produce it, all I have to do is be strong enough in Christ to *hold* the fruit He's producing in my life.

You know, looking back, I wonder how much fruit I didn't "hold" because I was so busy trying to "produce" fruit on my own. I wasn't focused on what God was doing in my life, I was focused on what I was doing for Him. Trust me on this, the difference between the two in theory and in practice are *huge!*

The funny thing is, since I've stopped trying to produce fruit for Him, fruit in abundance of abundance has come into my life. In my books, in my kids, in my marriage, in our finances. Things I used to work so hard to accomplish (which never seemed to work out) are suddenly heaped upon me in blessing after blessing. I am convinced it's because I stopped trying to produce and started being content to hold that this change has come about.

So, as I said before, consider this simple yet profound modification in the way you define "bear." It may well change your entire life. (2006)

A Reason to Pray

Recently I was reading Nancy Stafford's *Beauty by the Book*. She pointed out something I hadn't thought of. Words associated with Christ often start with the prefix re- as in renew, refresh, restore, resurrection. Words associated with Satan, however, often start with either de- or dis- Destroy, discourage, disappoint, despair, depression. Re- means to bring back to the original state. Even though as a root word de means "of" as in desire—of the Father; as a prefix de- or dis- means away from, down, or separation or negation, which pretty much describes Satan.

Of course you know this to be true in your own experience. When you're with Christ, you feel a sense of rebirth and rejuvenation of your soul. When you're hanging with the devil, there's a lot of disease, disappointment, disillusionment, distrust, and despair. You know the signs when the devil is working on you. Now you can let that disempower you—as he is trying to do. In fact, Ms. Stafford sums up Satan's agenda in one very powerful sentence. "His sole purpose is to isolate and destroy us, either emotionally or physically." That's about as succinct a goal statement for Satan as I've ever read. Isolate and destroy. And I'm quite sure you know how that feels.

So, like I said, you can use the knowledge that Satan is working to destroy you as a reason to give up, quit, surrender, and let him take you down. Or, you can recognize what's going on and use it as a reminder to fight back.

Now you and I both know that Satan is a wily little booger who will use our greatest weaknesses to crack us in two—or several hundred—pieces. We also know that on our own fighting him, we are sunk. That's why at some point in the past we accepted Christ's work on the cross on our behalf so that Satan no longer can lay claim to our lives.

Great and good.

But what about when it feels like Satan is winning in the here and now? What about when he uses those bills we haven't paid to tell us that we are worthless dust, unworthy of God's love much less His help?

What about when Satan throws our past sins up in our face? "Yeah, you think you are so holy, but what about when you…?" From personal experience, he's good at this. He knows what we most fear. He knows what angers we harbor deep inside. He knows what we haven't forgiven, and he uses these things to eat away at us, pecking at us like chickens do a sick chicken until it dies.

Finally, after many years of searching, I have found a weapon that combats Satan right where he's working. It's effective. It's easy. And best of all, it gets quick results.

It's remembering this phrase, "This is a reason to pray."

God drives Satan insane. In fact, Satan cannot be where God is. Better, Satan doesn't *want* to be where God is.

A friend of mine was having financial trouble. She had creditors calling who did not have a claim on the payment they were requesting, but that didn't stop them from calling—every day. At home, at work, on her cell phone. Despite getting solid legal advice that she did not owe this money, they kept calling. The situation was sending her into panic attacks and had anxiety wrapped over her like a wet blanket.

When she finally told me what was going on, as we talked, the Holy Spirit whispered the answer to me. "Tell her to use this as a reason to pray." Not in general terms, like at night saying, "Please, God. Take this away." But directly.

As crazy as this is going to sound, I have now seen the following work miracles not just in this situation but in others. When the thoughts come (or the creditor call comes in, or the angry co-worker shows up, or the ex-husband calls), in your spirit say, "Oh, thanks, Satan. You're right. I need to pray about this. Bless you for reminding me… Thank You, God, for being in my life and for showing me Your best way to handle this. Be with me Holy Spirit. I give this situation to You. You are the most awesome friend I have! Thanks."

Let me tell you. Satan does NOT want to be the reason you

remember God. Remember the dis- words mean separation, away from, negation. He wants to separate you from God, to negate the good God is doing in the world. It drives Satan crazy to be the *reminder* that God is present and all you have to do is put the situation in God's hands to handle. And it's become very clear to me that Satan will pull up stakes and RUN from a situation where you do this.

You can even get more specific in the salutation you use for the minions Satan has sent to torment you. "Oh, fear, thanks. You're right. I need to pray about this. Bless you for reminding me."

Oh! I can hear the demons cartwheeling away from the situation even as I write. They have no power where God is, and an aside, they *hate* to be blessed! It's quite fun actually because you are learning to spread love even to your enemies. You will feel better and more at peace before you ever even get to the point of beginning to handle whatever is going on.

"Oh, thanks, Satan. You're right I need to pray about this. Bless you for reminding me."

Use Satan as your reason to pray, and in no time, he won't be lurking around your doorstep. Try it. You'll see what I mean.
(2006)

The Light

Your word is a lamp to my feet and a light for my path. Psalm 119:104

My dad always says that God doesn't put the light on your head so you can see way out into the future, He puts it at your feet so you can see the next step. While doing a walk recounting Jesus' journey to Calvary, I was with a large group of women. The walk began at dusk and continued as the light around us faded and slowly vanished.

The leaders had given each of us a battery-operated candle. A single light. I hadn't used mine most of the trip—preferring to walk the pseudo-journey up the Via Dolorosa in the dimming light as the world shut itself off around me.

Then as we rounded the curve after Jesus was crucified and on the way to see Him laid in the tomb, I realized that the older lady next to me was holding her candle closer to the walkway in an apparent attempt to see so she would not stumble. Immediately I took my candle out of my pocket and turned it on to help.

Unfortunately those candles were made to inspire the soul—not to light darkened walkways. My mind immediately said, "Gee, Stace, fat lotta good your puny little candle did." At that moment from directly behind me, someone turned on a mega-watt flashlight, and the whole walk was clearly visible.

In that instant, I got it. I don't have to light the whole way for those around me. All I have to do is turn my candle on, and Jesus' light will be right there to back me up. I simply must have the courage to believe in His light rather than my own so that I never think that I have to do it all myself. It was a lesson I needed to hear, and one I'm eternally glad He sent me on a walk through the gift He gave me. (2004)

The Gifts

Since reading Brennan Manning's *The Ragamuffin Gospel,* the meaning of the gifts of the Holy Spirit has suddenly come alive for me. Prior to reading about how grace can transform your life, I was already pretty solid in "letting Him do it." As a reformed control-freak, I had made a conscious choice to stop trying to control everything. I took my hands off the wheel and said, "God, You take my life where You want it to go."

It didn't take long before I could see how much better He put things together in my life. I could see how He put the people I most needed in my life, how He arranged meetings and "coincidences" to guide me in where I was supposed to go, how He formed a relationship seemingly for one purpose even though He had something much bigger in mind. However, it wasn't until Manning's book that I understood that the Holy Spirit was not "out there." It was "in here." In me.

It was literally God's Spirit in my heart, in my body, in my spirit. Wow! Did that understanding open doors!

I had always been taught about the gifts of the Holy Spirit—wisdom, knowledge, understanding, fortitude, right judgment, fear of the Lord, and piety. However, after letting the Holy Spirit not just direct my paths but begin to live through me, I have come to really understand these gifts in a new light.

A friend of mine is teaching a 7th grade Sunday school class. She came one day depressed because during the past Sunday's class her personal life had interfered with her teaching life. She said, "I just think I failed them." I then asked her if she had put the day's class in the Holy Spirit's hands. "Yes." To which, I asked, "Do you think the Holy Spirit can fail?" A long pause. "No."

"Then if you've put the situation in the Holy Spirit's hands, and

He is living through you, can you fail?"

It was the first time I had ever put it in those words even for myself, but at that moment, I got it. The more I put my life in His hands and let Him take control in situations instead of me trying to control them based on my meager knowledge and understanding, the more I see that nothing is impossible. Even if something looks like a failure to me, He has a plan.

When you let go and let the Holy Spirit take control, no longer will you have "I should've said but I didn't" or "I would've, but I was afraid." When He speaks to your heart, you learn to listen and to do and to say. Better than that you begin to let *Him* listen and do and say through you, and when that happens, the gifts that follow are more amazing than you can ever imagine! (2006)

Prove It!

You are of God, little children, and have overcome them, because He who is in you is greater than he who is in the world. –1 John 4:4

We all know the types, those people we encounter on a daily basis who feel they have to prove to everyone around them how important they are. They may be a boss, a co-worker, a spouse, a child, a friend, or just someone we happen to know. But whoever they may be, they have a way of getting under our skin with their constant need to make everyone else know they are not to be taken lightly.

I call this the "I-am-important-because..." syndrome. Now, of course, there are a myriad of ways to fill in the blank inherent in that statement. I am important because... I have money, I have power, I have the right car or the right clothes, I pay for dinners or gifts, my name is this, my skin color is that, I have x number of kids, or ex-husbands, or bank accounts, I am a banker, lawyer, teacher, businessman; I give to charity; I'm saved, I'm a (fill in the blank) Catholic, Church of Christ, Mormon, Baptist, Methodist, Pentecostal, etc. or I'm not a (fill in the blank) Catholic, Church of Christ, Mormon, Baptist, Methodist, Pentecostal, etc., I went to college, I have a house on the lake, and on and on and on...

Look closely, and you will see that all of these statements have one thing in common: they are all designed to separate the speaker from the listener. They are designed to divide. Division is the desire of the ego. It says, "For me to have worth, I must diminish your worth." To me, there is no greater destructive force on earth than this mentality, and yet it runs rampant in our society.

In contemplating the storyline of a book that I wrote and trying to find ways to describe the undercurrents that run through the book, I realized that this is exactly what the characters are doing. The two main characters, Jaxton and Ami, are in an all-out battle with themselves to prove that they are in fact worth something to themselves, their families, and to the world. Because of this, even small tasks that they undertake become massive struggles.

One character, Jaxton, follows the "I am important because I have power" line of thinking. He uses that power to walk over people repeatedly. Truth be told, he himself has been walked over and dismissed by his own family, and he is desperate to prove to his ego that he is worth something. Ami, on the other hand, is a young woman reaching for a dream that she knows will never come true and thus will only prove once and for all that she is exactly what she feels she is in her heart: a failure. Against the persistent drag of the rational side of her ego, she works determinedly to the point of exhaustion trying to prove that her dreams matter, that she deserves to be successful, that she can make something work. The only problem is, she doesn't really believe this although she does her very best to prove to everyone around her that it is in fact the truth.

There is a counter-point character to these two, Jaxton's grandfather. Once I started thinking about him, the answer of why he was so different stood out clearly. He doesn't answer, "I am important because…" Instead, he has come to the realization that, "I am important." Period. And his actions are a consequence of that thinking (not the means to prove it).

He is generous not to prove how wonderful he is but because it's a natural outgrowth of the fact that he wants to share what he has with others. He is helpful and kind not so that others will be impressed but because that is what's in his heart, and there is a big difference.

When I was a teacher, there were always students who were less than respectful to the faculty and administration. I would see my fellow teachers go into fits of rage that these students would not give them the respect they deserved. To be honest, these students rarely bothered me. Why? Because my worth was not tied up in what they thought of me. I knew that as a child of the Most High God, I had worth, and I was important—regardless of what they thought.

We are not trying to please people, but God…
—1 Thessalonians 2:4

The other side of this coin is that I did not have to prove my worth to anyone. I wasn't on a power trip like some of my fellow teachers. I didn't have to run a student down to make myself feel better. I was there to help a student begin where they were and reach for the highest accomplishments they could achieve.

That mentality made me a successful teacher, but now I realize how it works in my life every day even now that I am no longer in the classroom. My marriage is stronger because of it, and it is only when I delve into trying to prove how "important I am" that it goes off track. In my business life, my employees don't have to tiptoe around wondering if they are going to hurt my feelings or provoke me because my feelings and moods are not based on external influences. They are based on the fact that God thinks I'm all right, and I don't have to prove that to anyone else.

My son, with humility have self-esteem; prize yourself as you deserve. Who will acquit him who condemns himself? Who will honor him who discredits himself? —10 Sirach 26-27

So, I challenge you to look around your life. In what areas are you fighting to prove you are worth it? And who around you is doing the same thing? For both sides, there's a simple answer to get out of the cycle of division and destruction. It is this: I am important, and so are you. Period. Work toward that, and you will be amazed at the peace that will befall the world you live in. (2003)

Coming Under

To begin with I hate green. At least I did. Let me explain. My mother's favorite color is green, and so everything in our house was green. *Everything.* The carpet was green. The walls were green. The ceiling was green. There was a green chair and green decorations on the walls. She even painted the outside of the house green once. She repainted it when her children vehemently protested.

That's why when she told me that she had wanted to dress me in a green outfit to bring me home from the hospital when I was born, I was less than thrilled. Green? The last thing I ever wanted to be in was *green.* But that story seemed to always follow me growing up. Every birthday, she would remind me about that little soft, green outfit she had dreamed of bringing me home in.

Of course, she always had good reasons to love green. Among them: green means growth, health, life. Plus, as she pointed out more than once, even money is green.

I never bought it. I still hated green. Then I went on retreat.

While on retreat, green began following me. Although the theme colors of the retreat were blue (my fav), yellow, purple, AND green, everything I got was green.

I got a green notebook, a green songbook, even a green cross. I was like, "What is going on here?" My tablemate asked what was up, and I explained the green thing, adding, "I can't figure out why green. I hate green. What is God trying to tell me?" She said, "Well, green is what helps flowers to bloom, and from what I've seen, your calling is helping others to bloom."

Suddenly green didn't seem nearly so bad. In fact, that was just a cool way to look at what I had been coming to see about myself. Finally, being green was an idea I could get behind.

Then on Sunday morning we were at the front of the church getting ready to sing our theme song. My family, sitting in the back of the church, had brought signs. One of my friends pointed this out. They had big "We love you, Mom" signs and were waving them for all they were worth.

I smiled. Then just behind me, one of my tablemates said, "Look. They're green!" She was right. Our theme song started, and two lines into it, I couldn't sing for the tears.

Hearts unfold like flowers before Thee
Praising Thee their Son above.

At that moment, I got it. I finally understand why green had been following me my whole life. Then today came along. It's been nearly three years since that Sunday when I stood on the steps of the church and had that moment. But if you follow God very much at all, you know the threads that really mean something run not just in one moment, but for a lifetime.

Today, I was reading an exposition on Ephesians 5. You know, the one that talks about a wife being subject to her husband. The discussion illuminated the term "to come under" as in she will "come under" the authority of her husband.

I had always taken "come under" to mean "put your will aside or under his." However, this book pointed out how the terminology in this verse is also used as Christ comes under the church, and the church comes under Christ.

It pointed out that the "coming under" was not about being dominated but rather about willingly coming under someone to give them support and to build them up.

In short, it's about being green.

You "come under" someone to be green for them—to support them, nourish them, build them up, so that they can bloom the way they were always meant to..

Personally this was as big of a revelation as green for me. I think I'm going to make my new goal that of coming under everyone God sends my way—my husband, my children, my friends, other writers, those I teach.

You see, coming under is not an act of weakness. It is a position in which the strength God has put in you can be accessed by the flowers blooming above.

That's cool. It's as cool as being green.

Turns out my mom was right all along. Go figure. (2007)

God Bless Wendell

If you live with your eyes open for the opportunities God plants in your path, you just might get lucky enough to realize they are there before they aren't. By "opportunities" I don't mean "circumstances" or "fortuitous occurrences for you to get ahead." No, I mean people.

See, in this life, you don't have to learn only from your own experiences. In fact, if you're smart, you won't. If you're smart, you'll recognize the opportunities God gives you to learn from the experiences of others while they're still with you.

Wendell was one of my opportunities.

On the surface we were nothing alike. He was a 60-plus-year-old money manager who had done quite well for himself and his family. I once heard him tell the story of paying $80,000 cash for a house when he moved from Chicago to the Texas Panhandle. That wasn't a boast. It was Wendell, a straight shooter, who had learned enough about life to have it working for him instead of the other way around.

That's why I'm sure plenty of people thought he was nuts to take a nearly-no-paying job in a little private school that was deathly close to closing its doors. In fact, I later learned that during one particularly bad month, Wendell used his own money to pay the teachers' salaries until a grant came in to keep us floating for the next month

At the time I was a young, idealistic, first-year teacher who was doing everything I could to make a difference in my students' lives. It was an uphill battle. Not because of the kids but because of the jaded resignation around me.

On one side was the camp that vowed we would save them all – whether they wanted to be saved or not. On the other was the camp that said they were all hopeless so why bother?

I suppose that's why I first started going into Wendell's office – well, that and the fact that without a classroom of my own, I needed the table in his office to get anything done.

To this day I don't remember how our talks started. I don't even remember our first formal meeting. But by the third month of school, we were fast friends and partners on the same team. For hours and hours some nights after school we would sit and talk. Him behind a desk stacked with work; me with my briefcase full of work at my side. Both talking as if we had absolutely nothing else in the world to do.

More than once I remember knocking the back of my head against the door behind my chair, mostly in frustration over how complicated everyone else was making things. We talked about everything, Wendell and I. The state of the school. Finances. The way things were out-of-control and getting worse. What we could do about it and what we couldn't. We talked about life, and how it was best lived. We discussed faculty members and how some didn't seem to hold anyone accountable for anything and how others would jump a student with no provocation whatsoever. And we talked about the hierarchy above us.

That's how I learned a valuable lesson that I carry with me to this day. Now one thing about Wendell, he didn't look like he had a lot of money. He didn't look like he had much of anything at all. In fact, he looked a lot like an older version of Mr. Rogers. He wore the sweaters and everything. However, despite appearances, Wendell was no one's doormat. That was obvious to anyone who really knew him, but somehow the bishop missed that little detail.

One night, during a heated debate at a school board meeting, Wendell stood up to the bishop (to the absolute horror of the principal) when everyone else was cow-towing to a very bad decision he had made for the school. In no uncertain terms Wendell told the bishop that he was wrong and that the decision he had made was the dumbest one Wendell had ever been witness to. The next day back in the office, the mortified principal stormed into the office and demanded, "How could you say something like that to the bishop?"

Wendell's response? "Because he was wrong. Just because you put 'Bishop' or 'President' or 'Senator' or 'Principal' in front of someone's name, doesn't give them the right to run over everybody else, and if they're wrong, I'm going to say they're wrong. Bishop or no bishop."

Now Wendell wasn't advocating muting against authority. He was simply pointing out that with authority comes the responsibility to do what's right, and if you don't, you deserve to be called on it—no matter who you are or what your title happens to be.

Two years later, when I was expecting my first child, I made the decision to resign at the school year's end so I could stay home and raise my family. One night during one of our talks I confessed that I had begun to waver in my decision. I told Wendell that I felt like I was letting the school down by leaving. "Ah, Staci," Wendell said like a patient, omniscient grandfather, "you're destined for much bigger things than this place."

Sadly, Wendell's no longer with us. He died before I ever even started writing my books, and yet I often wonder if he could see now even back then. Now my books and words have touched myriads of souls that I will most likely never even meet this side of Heaven. In short, I have been granted some authority, some influence in other people's lives—an opportunity that I never could have imagined having back then. And I've got to tell you, I take that responsibility very, very seriously. Why? Because once a very wise man took the time to teach me the importance of shouldering the authority you are given, of doing the right thing no matter what your station in life happens to be, and of using the "title" you are given for the good of all—not just to show your own power and place in the world.

For that lesson alone I say, "God bless Wendell." (2004)

Assignment Complete

Long before I read Bruce Wilkinson's *The Prayer of Jabez*, I knew that people were sent into my life for a reason. I had seen too many head-snapping turns lead me right into someone who needed me (and often into someone who I really needed) to believe anything else. A segment of society that my life kept leading me to was teenagers. Many of these posed some of my most incredible "assignments."

One such young lady was a family member who, from what I saw, worked harder than any single other person I've ever met. Although not a natural in schoolwork, she took that fact as a personal challenge. All through high school, she would ask me for help if she ran into an obstacle that even she found daunting. For example, we watched *Hamlet* all day one day because she was studying it and not "getting it." We read and revised countless papers so they weren't just good but the best they could be. Then toward the end of her high school days, our attention turned to college—how she was going to get in, what she was going to take, and most of all, how she was going to pay for it.

Her parents were far from being independently wealthy and with two younger children in the family, were afraid what little money was available might run out long before their daughter got through. So in her senior year, we began working to find scholarships she could apply for, filling out forms, and reading and re-reading application essays so that she would have the best shot she could get at the money that was available to her.

Not long before graduation, she had an interview for a scholarship—her first formal interview, and she was nervous. One night her mother called me worried about how this interview would go. Because the young lady was going up against students from the more "elite" schools in the district, her mother was particularly worried that her daughter had nothing suitable to wear. Seeing her point, I quickly made the decision that we would just have to do something about that. I called the young lady and offered to take her shopping. We would get a couple of outfits and because I already knew she wanted to do something more sophisticated with her hair, I offered to take her to my salon and have it done, too.

Although it sounds "elegant," it really wasn't that big of a deal. In fact, in all, it wasn't that big of an investment. A hundred or so for the outfits. Thirty or so for the hairstyle. Not a big deal to me, but boy did that investment pay off!

Strangely enough she didn't land that scholarship, but that day gave her a confidence boost that helped her get many more scholarships. True-to-form, she went to the college of her choice, worked her brain to the max, and is now set to graduate with a better-than-3.6 point and a degree in Industrial Engineering, plus she is only one of six students to ever graduate with honors from that program. Not only that, but she has already landed a far-above-average-paying first job and will graduate with no debt. Amazing.

Although I know I will continue to help this young lady when and if I am needed, I realize now that this "assignment" is completed. Peeking over the horizon now are two more—one, to impress upon Assignment One the need for her to find another young woman to "help out" and two... to find a new assignment!
(2003)

2

On Family

You can't go wrong when you love others.
(Romans 13-10, TMB)

128

Funny how God sets things up—even when we don't take the time to notice. My biggest concern was leaving my children for three days to go on the retreat.

Now, I knew they would survive three days without me. I also knew they were in good hands. That wasn't the point. The point was that I wanted to be there to put them to sleep, to wake them up, to sit in the chair and snuggle with them every morning. I wanted to hold them and remind them that I love them just in case they had forgotten since the last time I told them. Instead here I was missing them and wondering how I would ever make it three days without them.

I was at peace, knowing that God would keep them for me, but I still knew I would miss not having them right there with me. I went anyway, heavy heart and all.

When I got the key to my room, I dutifully memorized the number even as I carried and walked with my kids down the hall so they could see where Mommy was going to stay. 128. 128. 128. Stefani's hand in mine. Andrew in my arms. Kayla holding onto my pant leg. Together, we all stepped into the room, looked around, and then it was time to go.

The evening passed. We separated as I kissed them. After a few activities, we were allowed to go back to our rooms. I took out my key and saw "128" stamped on it.

128. Why did that number sound so familiar and why had I been assigned that room and not say 122? I've come to know that when I notice something like that, it's usually because God's trying to give me a message through it. I had noticed, so I knew there was a message there that God was trying to point out to me.

As I looked at the key, I thought, "Huh, Stefani is 8. Maybe that's why it sounds so familiar." Then I looked a little closer. "Andrew's one! One and eight. Andrew and Stefani, but where's Kayla?"

Number sense training kicked in at that point. I knew there was a 5 there somewhere, but that 2 was all wrong. Then I saw it.

$1 + 2 = 3$ and $8 - 3 =$ You guessed it! FIVE!

So I got the right room. I know because God gave me the key I needed to hold onto all weekend. It was a nice reminder that He's watching out for all of us—me and my kids. If we ever doubt that, I know without question that He will put a key in our hand to remind us. (2004)

The Picture

We had a lot of pictures taken at our wedding—a lot of pictures. We had two photographers and two videographers, so there weren't many pictures that we missed. However, out of all those pictures, there is one perfectly perfect one.

It wasn't a staged one. It wasn't one I had on my infamous "list" to have taken. I didn't know it had been taken. I didn't even see this one until nearly a month after we'd been married. Yet is it my favorite of all of them. Why? Because in one single image our relationship was captured—frozen forever on Fuji Photo Film.

They say a picture is worth a thousand words, but I'll try not to use quite that many to explain it. In the picture I'm doing what I'm always doing—directing traffic. Since it was taken during the photo session following our wedding and since we didn't see each other before the wedding and since my husband's immediate family had 26 people in it at the time, there was a lot of traffic to direct. There were certain pictures that I wanted, and we had a small window of opportunity to get them taken.

In short, I was occupied.

The picture shows me, looking off-camera, pointing to someone and explaining what I want done. My dress that day didn't make doing things myself an option, so I had to rely on everyone else. It's easy to see in the image that I'm intent on getting whomever it is to do whatever it is I want done immediately.

As funny and point-blank as I am what makes the photo poignant is what my newlywed husband is doing. What's that? Exactly what he always does—he's taking care of me.

As my attention is elsewhere, he's standing there patiently picking tiny pieces of birdseed out of my hair. The thing is, he looks like he's got not another thing in the world to do, not one other thing to worry about. Amazing. Us in living color.

Many, many times since that photo was taken we've relived that moment. Me taking care of others, me ordering the world around us, him patiently taking care of me. Now, twelve years later, during the present incarnation of our relationship, I'm the one out there trying to learn new things. I'm the one out there taking us out of our comfort zone, pulling us in directions we never could have seen or imagined at that moment.

But the thing is, I can take those chances, chase those dreams because I know with no doubt that he will always be right there, patiently keeping me together. It's how we've always been. I have the proof. (2003)

Raising Ragpickers

The savior in Og Mandino's *The Greatest Miracle in the World* is a mysterious old man with an affinity for what he calls humanity's rags. In the story Og is the rag—an ambitious, successful magazine publisher who is burning out faster than a candle in water. The irony is that his magazine is about Success, but he's become increasingly dissatisfied with everything in his life. And then his ragpicker shows up.

It's not hard to see that our world does a good job of making millions upon millions of people feel like rags. We are washed up, tired, empty, and worn out. It is as if the human rag pile is ten miles high and getting higher by the moment. It would seem to be evident that the world needs more ragpickers—those people who are not only not on the rag heap, but who can help those who are on it to get off.

After reading *The Greatest Miracle in the World*, I determined for myself that I would be a ragpicker to the best of my ability. What I soon learned is that as a role model for my three kids, I am daily showing them how to be ragpickers. That was not my original intention, but it's working.

My oldest daughter came home from school one day, and we were talking about recess. She was telling me about the "groups" the kids had formed. One was the cheerleading group. One was the acting group, and on and on. She was telling me how she had been playing with one little girl who had gotten thrown out of her group for not following all the rules.

I asked her what they did, and she said, "Oh, we just sat under the tree and dug for worms." I, feeling my parental concern for her well-being, said, "Well, Stef, what group are you in?" To which she replied, "Oh, I'm not in a group. I just play with whoever the others don't want to play with."

Of course, I want my child to feel a part of things, and so I said, "Don't you want to be in a group?" She just shrugged and said, "Not really. There's always someone to play with because the groups are always mad at somebody."

It was then that I realized she was a ragpicker! She wasn't desperately trying to be a part of what the world said she had to be. No, she was content to be herself and to pick up the rags until they felt loved enough to go back to the group.

Since then, I have seen on more than one occasion the respect her peers have for her. One little boy at a birthday party told my husband, "Stefani must have never been around any mean person because it doesn't matter what happens, she has never been mean to me." (This was a little boy with severe ADHD that the teacher were in complete exasperation how to handle. One teacher told me she had put Stefani by him because Stef could deal with him when no one else could.)

Then there was another little boy in her class who was a bit slow with learning. That year the teacher told me that she had put Stefani by this little boy because Stef just naturally helped him when he got lost on the instructions. The teacher said, "She is just so patient with him. It amazes me."

The other night we were at the school for an open house, and we were hanging out talking. One little boy said to Stefani, "You were saying the other day how much you were screaming about something. That's weird. I just can't picture you screaming about anything. Stefani. Screaming. They just don't even go together."

I can't say that I did it, but I'd like to give some credit to Mr. Mandino for helping me to decide to be a ragpicker myself. I think it was the key to teaching me to raise ragpickers, and I will forever be grateful for that lesson. (2006)

Patience

Ever since my girls were very little, I've tried to teach them patience. I well remember getting them to count to ten when we had to wait for something. I would tell them, "Count real slow." If they counted "too fast" because I knew they would be finished before whatever we were waiting for was, I would say, "No, that's too fast. You have to start over."

It was a game, and it worked. It gave them something to think about other than what they so desperately wanted. By the time they got to ten, it was ready.

This Christmas I found out that those early lessons with my girls are paying off. My girls, now 9 and 5, were at Grandma's house Christmas morning. They awoke, as most children do on Christmas morning, very early.

When Grandma got up at 8:30 after a late night of playing games and visiting, she found the two of them in the living room looking at the wrapped presents and whispering. Not a box had been touched.

Grandpa got up at nine, and they ate some breakfast. Daddy got up about ten. By that time, the girls had sorted the boxes into Stefani's stack, Kayla's stack, Andrew's stack, etc. and still they were sitting patiently – examining, shaking, holding, discussing, but never opening.

Daddy, being the teasing guy that he is, tried to talk them into opening "just one." But they flatly refused until Mommy and Andrew could be there.

At 10:45, their baby brother woke up, and after a short discussion they decided they'd better wake Mom up because there was no telling how long she might sleep if they didn't.

The first I knew of any of this was when the four of them

appeared at my bedside saying, "Mom, wake up. We just can't wait anymore."

I don't know how long my mother will be alive, but I can guarantee she will forever marvel about those few hours on a bright Christmas morn when her two young granddaughters showed her the meaning of real patience. (2005)

3

On Being

The authority the Master gave me is for putting people together, not taking them apart. (2 Corinthians 13:10, TMB)

The Whole He Made

Every story is different
But every walk the same.
Every piece, every step
designed to show the One
Who creates the main.

No one can see from the outside
Sometimes we can't see from within
But He can see us always,
And see us He does
in each and every moment

Not as the disparate, incomprehensible
pieces that the world sees,
But as the perfectly placed pieces
of the whole He made,

And the whole He made is perfect,
The whole He made is good.
The whole He made is mighty.
The whole He made is glorious.

You are the whole He made.

(2004)

Believe

Believe that God can do all things, and He will.

Believe that you are never alone for He is always there.

Believe what you need will always be supplied for it will be.

Believe you are rich for you are. After all, you are His child, and He owns the universe.

Believe what you ask shall be given unto you, it will.

Believe everything is possible for in Him Who is everything, it is.

Believe there are angels right now working on your behalf, doing His work, in His way, in His time, for His purposes and because of His tremendous love for you, for that is true.

Believe you are loved for you are—today, tomorrow, and for eternity.

(2005)

4

On Living

Do your best in the job you received from the Master. Do your very best. (Colossians 4:17, TMB)

The Breaking Point

I cannot explain why this is exactly, but I know it to be true. God is giving me a crash course in breaking points. I don't mean little breaking points like you broke a nail. I mean soul-crushing, gut-wrenching, crying-in-anguish breaking points where you just scream out, "Why, God? Why? This is so unfair!"

There have been breaking points in my own family, in my friends, and in people I am just coming to know. Break downs, breaking hearts, broken lives... so many hurts, so much suffering that I can't help but ask the Lord, "Why? Why would You allow this? Why? These are Your children whom You love in ways we cannot fathom, and yet You allow these things to happen. Why?"

As I have often written, many lessons in the physical realm are present, I believe, to explain things in a deeper, spiritual realm. Thus it is with a broken bone. Most people know that when a bone breaks and is reset, the healed part is stronger than the rest of the bone. The healing actually makes the bone stronger than before it was broken.

Does a broken bone hurt? As the owner of two previously broken bones, I can attest that the answer is: YES! Is it fun to have a broken bone? NO! Would I ever on my own understanding choose to have a broken bone? NO! And yet... And yet...

Life throws things at us, and if life is taking a rest, the world gets into the act. Disease, death, heartache, addiction, divorce, abuse, the suffering of loved ones, the pain of others that we can't fix no matter how much we want to. All of these are very real. And all in one way or another point to something broken, something that needs healing, some point in us that needs to be turned over to Him because just like a broken bone, we cannot heal it. He has to.

I have heard it said that "God never gives us more than we can handle." I've heard it, but I don't believe it. I think God does, in fact, give us more than *we* on our own can handle. Because if we could handle it, what need would we have of going to Him? If we could handle it, why would we ever have cause to get to know Him on the deepest levels, those levels where no one else knows us, those levels where we often don't even know ourselves? Those levels where our deepest fears reside. Those levels where our deepest sorrows lie.

As difficult as this sounds, I believe that like a good shepherd who will break the leg of a wandering sheep so that it will not get itself into more danger, God will in fact allow us to be pushed to the breaking point and then push once more so that we will break. Only when the bone is broken can it be healed and become stronger.

What needs broken in us the most? Our belief that we can do it? Our belief that we have to be "strong"? Our belief that these things He puts into our lives are somehow tests to see how strong we are? The reality is: He knows our breaking points—maybe better than we do. He knows the very things that will puncture our hearts so that we cry out to Him. He knows the things standing between Him and us, and He will break those things so that even in those areas we rely on Him.

Maybe our children are the one thing we cannot give over to Him. We feel responsible for them. We feel He gave them to us, and so we are to fix them to the best of our ability. And they break. They become willful. They leave the church. They go off the path. They run from His love and ours, and no matter what we try, we can't seem to get them back on track.

It's tough, but we have to learn to give them to God. Because what I can't do, He can.

Maybe it's our job or a co-worker. No matter what we try there is still angst and turmoil. Maybe it's time to turn that over to God. It's tough, but remember: I can't, but He can.

It sounds brutally cruel, but what I have found by walking with countless people through these breaking points is that it is only when they have hit bottom and found that all they had left was God, it was only there that they really found God.

Do I advocate having a breakdown simply so you can find God? No. But I think every little trial has the capacity to let us learn to lean on Him then, so that when the big trials come along we're already in practice.

May the places you feel broken begin to be healed even in this very moment, and may you give over those places that feel as if they might break right now. He will heal them. More importantly, He will give you peace through the process. He knows what we most need, and what we most need is Him. That's the lesson of every breaking point. (2006)

Short Term vs. Long Term Thinking

It's a human fact. We want what we want when we want it. Short term thinking. It's the hole in many of our boats. The one that will eventually take us all the way to the bottom if we don't change it.

For reasons I will never fully understand this side of Heaven, I have always been a long-term thinker. Most of the biggest decisions of my life were made thinking long-term. I remember the decision to stay pure for marriage. Yes, there were many adamant, compelling reasons not to, but I always asked myself, "How am I going to convince my future kids that this is an important element of life if I don't hold it important in my life now?"

In going to college, I knew the best choice was to move another hour and a half away from my boyfriend so I could concentrate on schoolwork. Not an easy decision, but one I will forever be glad I made for what it taught me about myself, about him, and about our relationship. Is that the right decision for everyone? Probably not. But it was a conscious choice that in the long-term, for us, it was the best decision.

Long-term decisions are very rarely the easiest course of action. Many times they require sacrifice of what I want now. In the short term of course I wanted to spend more time with my boyfriend, but in the long term sacrificing some time together so we could be together on a firm foundation was more important.

I think too often we make decisions based on what looks good, feels good, seems good in the short term. We flirt with the cute guy because it's all in innocent fun. The long term consequences for our marriages don't enter into our thinking.

We go for that bag of potato chips or that large sundae because it sounds so good right now. Of course, it will come back to haunt us with pounds and health issues, but those are way out in the future, right? We let our short-term pleasure decide our long-term health, and it's killing many of us.

I challenge you today to look at your life. What decisions are you making in the short term that when you really take the time to look at what that decision will mean long term aren't supporting who you are or who you really want to be. Determine today to take two big decisions and begin to make them for the long-term rather than for the short term. Commit to doing the little things today that will bring about what you truly want.

If you don't, the pleasure you have in the short term will inevitably lead to pain in the long term. Get this decision right, and life will become vastly easier. (2006)

Rainbows

I've always loved rainbows, so this lesson was a little hard for me to learn. A few friends and I got together to sing—one of my favorite things to do. One of the songs we pulled out was about chasing rainbows. It said in effect that we're all just chasing pretty rainbows, but as pretty as they are, when we get there, they aren't what we thought they would be. Of course in the literal world, this is true. If you've ever tried to capture a rainbow, you know you can drive forever and never catch it. It changes, it moves, and then it disappears.

The concept of chasing pretty rainbows stayed with me as we continued to practice this song over the next several weeks, and I began to see how many rainbows I had been chasing. There was the rainbow of publication. The rainbow of success. The rainbow of achievement. The rainbow of others' approval and acceptance. Sometimes I got close. Sometimes I actually swiped my hand right through one. But always they would change, move, and then disappear.

Nearly instantly a new rainbow would appear on the vast plain of my life, and I would think, "Oh, I get it. It wasn't THIS rainbow that I really wanted at all. It was THAT one. Now if I can just figure out a way to get over *there*, then I'll be happy."

We all know about these rainbows. One is called education. If I just get through high school, then I'll be happy. If I just go to college, if I just get my masters, if I just, if I just… Then those rainbows start looking pale, and new rainbows appear. If I could just meet the man of my dreams, then life would be fabulous forever. Then it moves. If we could just get married… Again it moves. If we could just have kids… If he would just get this job, if I could just stay home, if we could just make enough to afford, if things weren't so busy, if we can just get through Christmas, if I just had enough work, if I didn't have so much work... Always those rainbows move.

First they are to the right and then to the left, backward, forward. But somehow those rainbows are never right here. Father Robert Barron in *Untold Blessings* calls it being scattered, and that's a very good word for it. Wherever you are, over there always looks better. Most frustratingly, sometimes over there is in several different places at once. You scramble and you scrape to reach that other rainbow so life will get better.

The truth is all of those rainbows are illusions. Getting a rainbow will never make life better. The only way life gets better is to have the Maker of the Rainbows with you right now. When you have Him, chasing rainbows that the world says are important becomes far less important to the point of non-existent. You realize that the rainbows will not make you happy. In fact they keep you frustrated and scattered as long as you believe they are the treasure you are searching for. Only He can bring you the peace you are so desperate to find.

Matthew 13:44 tells the story of the man who found a great treasure in a field. He went and sold all he owned so he could buy that field. The truth is the great treasure is Christ, and giving up all you own involves giving up striving for all those things the world says you have to have, all those pretty rainbows. The only true rainbow is the Rainbow Maker. So seek Him first, and all the other rainbows you most need will be added unto you. The best part is they will not require vast amounts of effort to reach. They will be "added" to your life.

It will be as if your whole life is filled with rainbows you never stopped long enough to really notice. The rainbows of the world are as smoke—inconsequential and hollow. The rainbows of God are real and eternal.

So which kind of rainbow do you have right now? Which one do you want? (2005)

Perfection—The Lie That Binds

I don't care who you are. You know that perfection stinks. If you are a perfectionist, you know as well as I do that no matter how hard you try, nothing is ever right enough. If you get within two feet of perfection in one area, there are three more right behind it to show you how imperfect you really are. Maybe, however, you are on the other side of that sword. Maybe you know someone who is perfect (not really, but they sure put on a good show). Of course, when you are around them, you can't help but feel less than no matter what you do.

Perfection is a piece of baggage I carried for a long time. It was heavy, and it was bulky. No matter what I did, how successful I was, I still heard Satan whispering, "Yes, but it isn't perfect." Of course, it wasn't perfect. God didn't make us perfect. If He had, there would've been no need for the cross and Calvary. In fact, I think that even Adam and Eve weren't perfect. I think even they had flaws, but before the fall, they also had something else—a deep understanding that God loved them just as they were no matter what.

I think that is one of the heaviest bags a perfectionist carries— the belief that no one could really love them if they aren't perfect. They spend their lives with their spirits in chains because of this. They hold onto the core belief that even God could not love someone so flawed. With this belief dogging their heels, they do their absolute level best to convince the world that they have no flaws.

Floors? They are spotless. Kids? They don't make mistakes. Dress? Ironed, pressed, creased. Life? Planned to the last minute. They have no worries, no fears, no problems.

In truth, fear is what drives their lives. Fear makes every decision, says every word, dictates every action.

That's what non-perfectionists looking in do not see. They do not see the fear, and so they assume there isn't any. They assume that there must be something wrong with them because they do feel fear. They assume that somehow they are less than because they can't be perfect like X.

Lies. It's all lies. Hideous, odious, spirit-crushing lies all around.

Dragging perfection through life is a cross that keeps getting heavier and heavier because the perfectionist can never be real. They can never let others see the truth because they know their perfection is a lie. So on top of perfection, the lies start building. To those looking on, these lies only exacerbate the guilt they feel, and so the lies add weight after weight to them as well.

There is a way to break through these lies, but it's not easy. It takes the perfectionist admitting the truth first to him or herself and then to others that they are not perfect. It is letting others see that their house isn't always in perfect order, that sometimes they are unorganized, that they have fears and worries just like everyone else. For those looking on, this requires being a soft place to fall, reiterating to the perfectionist that they are loved no matter what.

Either one can start the process, but it takes both to make it come full circle. The perfectionist must admit they are not perfect, and the others must admit that's okay. It's worth the work if you can ever get past the fear of jumping into real and leaving the fiction of perfection behind. (2005)

On Meaning

I recently read a book by Jeff VanVonderen which I highly recommend. It's called *Families Where Grace is in Place*. This book opened my eyes to a phenomenon I knew was there but could never put precise words to explaining. The concept is rather simple but very enlightening. It goes something like this.

Many of us were born into families, even Christian families, were Grace was not in place. Mr. VanVonderen calls these "Curse-ful Relationships." Curse-ful relationships are born when a person feels empty on the inside but tries to use the outside of themselves to make the world believe they are wonderful.

Another empty person sees the outside of this wonderful acting person and thinks that this is what they need to fix themselves. They too feel empty, and they think this other person will fill them up and make them feel good about themselves.

Of course the problem quickly becomes felt although very often is not "visible" to the participants. The spouses begin to realize that the other person has * gasp * flaws too, and so they begin to try to fix the other person. Their belief becomes, "I would feel better if he was better."

The reality is one empty spouse cannot fix or fill the other spouse enough so that they themselves will feel better. It will not work. Mr. VanVonderen then explains that these empty spouses attempt to find fill their emptiness with things outside themselves— ministries, work, money, accomplishments, and very often, ultimately children.

The children are meant to "fill" the emptiness. Here's a newsflash for those who don't know. Children don't fill the emptiness, what they often do is point it out in big neon letters! You want to know where you're flawed, where you lack patience and kindness, understanding and wisdom? Have a child!

Pretty soon these parents who feel so empty themselves pass that emptiness onto the child, and the whole cycle repeats.

I really learned a lot from Mr. VanVonderen's book, but it left me with a nagging hole. Although he tries to fill the hole, it comes across as more rules to follow and feel like a failure than a real solution. There was something in me that knew there was a better answer, but I didn't know what that was.

Then the Holy Spirit did a most remarkable thing. He led me to a book with the answer. Strangely, this book was written nearly 40 years before, but I believe it holds the key to transforming Curse-ful families into Grace-ful families.

Although not a religious tome, this book is chocked full of truly deep human understanding. Strangely I've had it on my bookshelf for far more than a year but had never read it. I had heard about it in many different contexts and had for years exhorted myself to read it, and still I hadn't. Now I understand why.

I don't think had I read it years ago that I would've put this piece with the VanVonderen book and come out with a true a-ha moment.

The book is by Victor Frankl, and it is called *Man's Search for Meaning*. Mr. Frankl spent World War II in a concentration camp. He saw men reduced from men of leisure with their masks firmly in place to men stripped of everything, right down to who they really were. In this stark environment, Mr. Frankl, being a psychiatrist prior to entering Auschwitz, observed the situation on a much deeper level than many who had the unfortunate fate to be prisoners there.

What did Mr. Frankl learn? That even in the most dire of circumstances some men will rise above and become true heroes and some will degenerate into the depths of depravity and despair. Now, you may think that classification—guards vs. prisoners; Capos (prisoners who got to be superior to regular prisoners) vs. regular prisoners—would divide the heroes from the malicious, but nothing could be further from the truth.

Over and over, Mr. Frankl points to guards who were kinder than their peers; Capos who tried to make the prisoners more comfortable and give them hope; and prisoners who went out of their way to lighten the load of their fellow men. Then with as great of precision, he would point to those on every level who used their position to tread on others, to shoot down their hopes, to make a mockery of their fellow man.

Mr. Frankl's experience allowed him the distinct opportunity to distill that what separates man from man is ultimately how he answers one question: What is *my* meaning in this life?

Rather than asking, "What is the meaning of life?" in general, which Mr. Frankl says is a pointless channel of inquiry, he says that to find the meaning of life, we must be willing to ask the question on a personal, individual level. And once we know our meaning (or some of our meanings), our circumstances cease to be a factor in our accomplishing that meaning.

Mr. Frankl points to three possible abstract meanings which man might choose:

1) achievements and accomplishments
2) finding someone or something to love
3) learning to take suffering and turn it to triumph—either by learning to live with it with your head held high, or by conquering it outright

There is far, far more to this fascinating book than I can discuss here, but I would like to suggest that Mr. Frankl's book is the illumination that fills Mr. VanVonderen's hole of how to have a Grace-ful life (and relationships that flow from that life).

Simply put, "What is my meaning in this life? What can I do that literally no one else who is alive now, in the past or in the future can ever do?"

Maybe the answer is to be a loving father or mother to the children you have. Maybe the answer is to write a story or a book that no one else can write. Maybe the answer is to play an instrument, take food to the homeless, visit the sick, write a song, build a bridge, build a house, be someone to talk with/a shoulder to cry on. Maybe the answer is to love a homeless animal, send a card to a friend, paint a picture, put together a computer program, teach a class, be a mentor, be a coach, be a friend…

Or maybe it's none of those, but one of a hundred million other things.

Take some time today to sit down and contemplate, "What is

my meaning in this life? What can I do that I alone was meant to do? What space can I fill that I was meant to fill?"

Find your meaning, the true desire of your heart, pursue it, and grace will fill every empty space inside you to overflowing. (2006)

Burning the Boats

I have the feeling that this lesson could change my life in many, many ways. It's something I just came across yesterday. By today I had forgotten it until I turned on my copy of Andy Andrews' excellent DVD *The Seven Decisions*. If you have a chance, get this DVD. It is worth every penny.

The lesson we are tuning ourselves to today is that of Cortez, the great conqueror. Now as Mr. Andrews tells it, Cortez took 11 boats, nearly 500 men, weapons, and a deep desire to conquer the greatest treasure on earth. Although Cortez had hand-selected these men to come with him on his journey, part way across he realized many were your standard-fare naysayers.

They began saying to Cortez and each other, "We never should have come. This is crazy. No one has been able to take the treasure for 600 years. What makes us think we'll do any better?"

So by the time they arrived for the conquering part of the journey, Cortez pretty much knew he had a problem. These men were not 100% committed to this task. In fact, many of them would in all likelihood duck, cover, and run at the first sign of real trouble. Therefore, upon arrival at their landing spot, Cortez set up a series of talks about how great the treasure really was, how proud their families would be of them if they succeeded, how their names would be recorded in history.

When the last speaker had spoken and it was time to put their vision into action, Cortez took center stage. He motioned for them all to come forward to hear what he had to say, and they did. This was it. It was time. Cortez looked at them and said three simple words. "Burn the boats."

Burn the boats? What? He must be crazy! He must be out of his mind! What if things don't go well? What if we have to get out of here in a hurry?

But Cortez's orders were carried out, and the boats were burned.

Now think about how this applies in your life. Have you ever determined, "That's it. We've got to do something about this debt we're in." So you work on it—for about two days—until it gets hard, or you get bored, or maybe something comes up that you really just have to have. And you get back on the boat and head back where you came from.

Practically speaking, I'm trying to find ways to burn my boats. Losing weight is a goal of mine. It's a goal, and although in the past I have in fact burned the boats in relation to my weight, and subsequently attained the weight I wanted to be, this time I can't find the absolute commitment that it takes. Not just when I can, but every time. Every time I eat something or need to exercise. EVERY TIME.

In short I need to find a way to burn the boats. It has to be do it or die. Do it. Find a way. Make a way. But do it. I'm going to. Those boats need burned because the truth is the treasure of health IS worth it. The question is: How committed am I?

And so you don't think I've forgotten: How committed are you to conquering to attain your treasure? Burn your boats. Do it or forget it. As Yoda says, "Do or do not. There is no try." I think he must've been with Cortez, or maybe all the truly wise beings know this maxim.

I know it now, the question is: Will I use it?

Burn the boats. (2006)

My Money

We all operate under a myth, and that myth when acted upon and taken for truth can twist us into spiritual and emotional pretzels. Look around. There are a lot of spiritual/emotional money pretzels around. You know the types. The ones who spend every waking hour at work, chasing a dollar because their bank accounts say they are broke, and their lives reflect the fact that they really are.

To them, money, if not the answer, is at least something to be captured and horded. They believe their status in life is reflected both in the money they have/make and in the lifestyle they get to live. They throw money at houses to show how well they live. They throw money at cars and at things to fill the houses. It's a desperate attempt to make themselves feel better because in truth, they know how bad they feel. They know how empty they really are.

Debt piles up. Yes, monetary debt, but also spiritual debt and emotional debt. It all piles on top of them until seeing out seems impossible. You know these people. You may even know them very, very well. You may look at "their" pocketbook every day and wonder how "they" got into this mess.

Not long ago a friend of mine and I had an interesting conversation. It went like this. He had lent someone money—not a grand amount in the general scheme of things, but enough. Then this someone did not pay him back right away. After many months, this someone began to renovate his home, new tiles, new roof. It was making my friend completely crazy. They had been friends before the loan, and now their friendship was tilting on the great black hole of never again.

My friend came to talk, and the subject wound around to this situation. He was in knots over it. I mean looking for ways to get his money back some boarding on ridiculous, but the fact was, he was tied to that money.

After a few minutes, I said, "You act like that money is yours."

That stopped him cold. "It is mine. That's the point."

I shook my head. "That money is not yours anymore than the other money you have in the bank is yours. It's not. It's God's money, and once you get that, you can let go and realize that God will take care of it—you don't have to."

It wasn't long after that the loan was paid back, and life got much simpler for my friend. His own bank account has soared not because of anything he's done different—except maybe in his thinking.

We were talking again recently, and I commented about how funny it is to me that we are the children of the God of the universe, and we're scrambling after 50 cents. Do we really believe (as we act) that if we recognize Who this money really belongs to that He will repel the money that is already His? No, our God *attracts* good things TO Him. If He is *in us* and we are *in Him* then we should realize the money will naturally come to Him/us. It is a given.

Once it is in our possession and we understand that it is not *our* money, we can see the ways He wants us to use it for His purposes—like that loan to a friend. Am I saying don't pay back loans to friends? No. That would not be honoring God or His money. I'm saying if you hold your money in fists, realize that nothing more can get in.

Breathe. Let go of the erroneous belief that this money is yours. It is not. When you understand that, you will recognize and embrace the opportunities to help others that come your way. And rest assured, the opportunities will always be in proportion to what you have already been given. Remember, it's the Master's money. You do not have to be afraid of Him. You do not have to hold it and bury it and be afraid of it and for it. Rejoice! For every use of it that has His hand written on it—whether for your benefit or for someone else's—it will come back to your life like iron to a magnet.

Try it. See if I'm wrong. (2006)

Layers of Existence

Movies are fascinating. They have a way of conveying messages without us realizing we are getting the message. I first gained this understanding in college. I took a cinema class because I thought it would be fun and easy. But God had other plans.

There were 800 students in cinema class. Apparently a lot of people had the same idea I did. The only one in the room who didn't know this was supposed to be easy was the teacher. She had this strange idea that we were actually there to learn about movies. Go figure!

Where we started, I no longer remember, but through the course of the semester we learned every technique directors use to pull us into their work. We went through the meanings of various camera angles, how props are used, how sets are designed, how costumes are chosen, colors, music, layout, dialogue, blocking, movement, and on and on and on.

We were given the chance (read: assigned) to deconstruct various techniques in movies we watched. For example, say you chose to analyze the music, you then took notes on how music was used throughout the movie to evoke the emotion you had decided the director was trying to bring out. Then you wrote what you thought about that in a 500-word paper.

It was fun. Slowly but surely the lessons came together so that I could see how a movie director constructs a world in which what you see and hear transfers into making you feel a certain way and understand the characters on a deeper level than maybe even you realize. Does he want you to feel fear? Low, menacing music will pull fear right out of you. Does she want you to sense that a character is out of control? Cluttering the character's living space with a myriad of props will (even if you're not aware of it) add to that perception.

Many years after the cinema class, I began to use these lessons in constructing my books. I intuitively understood that you didn't have to tell the audience a character was a control freak if his suit was impeccable, his desk perfect, his apartment sparse but in fastidious order, his commands to others followed to the letter or else. All of these add up to a character bent on controlling his existence—even if I never said that outright.

I could do that without even really trying. It wasn't until a writing friend pinned me down to explain it to her that I came to the realization of the layers of existence.

Simply put: What happens in the physical realm gives us cues as to what is happening on the emotional and mental levels, which then have an underlying lesson in the spiritual realm. Now, stay with me here. This isn't hard, and it will make a tremendous difference in how you live your life once you get it.

For a long time I saw this pattern in books, but it wasn't until recently that I discovered it transfers to life as well. When things happened in real life, I began to ask, "Why?" just as I did when writing my books. Not in a negative sense as in "Why does this always happen to me?" but in a curiosity sense, "Why? What does this mean? Where are we going with this?"

That opened up a whole new understanding of life for me. I began to see how what happens in the physical realm necessarily opens a window to understand the emotional, mental, and spiritual realms.

An example that happened recently was a friend of mine who was talking about a control freak in her life. She lamented that he always has to be right, he wants everything perfect or it's horrible, and he makes her the "small one" so he can be the savior. Listening I said, "You know why, right?" She paused. "No. Why?"

"Because he feels out of control and less than, so he's holding the things he can control in a tight fist. That helps him feel like he's in control so he doesn't have to feel out of control." After only a moment's thought, she said, "You know what? You're right. I never thought of it like that."

You see, what was happening in the physical realm—his controlling behavior—held cues to his emotional and spiritual state of being wanting at all costs to feel in control of everything.

It happens with lessons as well. As things in real life happen, I often step back and ask, "Okay, what's the lesson in this?" Invariably as the layers peel away, the lesson becomes clear. In fact, a friend of mine who has recently begun doing this commented the other night:

"I used to think things just happened, and that was that. Now, I stop and think, 'Okay. Wait. There's a lesson here. What is it?' It takes me awhile sometimes, but when I really stop long enough to look, the lessons become clear."

I'm glad I took that cinema class because it taught me more about life than I ever would've guessed. (2005)

It's the Little Things

"The Lord is with you, while you are with Him; and if you seek Him, He will be found of you." --2 Corinthians 15:2

The other day my sister called me at noon. I wasn't expecting the call. In fact, I had a whole day of plans already mapped out. But she was in town with her children and she needed a place for them to eat where she could feed her baby. There was no thought to the decision, "Sure, come on over."

In this world today, too many people miss this simple yet powerful lesson. In fact, in the hustle of life, I have been every bit as guilty of skimming over this lesson as anyone. But the lesson is still there: Life's bonds are not forged in the big, important moments. They are forged in every single passing moment that we so readily take for granted.

Years ago I gave a graduation speech to a class of seniors who I had taught every morning for an hour and a half. You would've thought that they would've been tired of hearing me talk, but they asked me to give their send off speech. Here is the crux of what I told them:

It is not the big decisions which ultimately determine where you end up in this life. It is what you decide to do that morning when you wake up, look at the clock, and really do not want to go to class that will decide where your ultimate destination lies. Because it is in that moment that the true nature of your true character is laid out before you. Are you a person who completes what they sign up to do to the best of your ability? Or are you a person who skates by and does only those things that you have to do or the things others will notice if you don't do them?

The answers to those questions decide far more than you think. In the beginning you may be the only one who notices how many times you don't follow through with the little things. Eventually everyone will be able to see the big things you failed to do because you were not reliable with the smallest. And in the end, you will be judged for the big things and the little things, so they are not to be taken lightly.

This is not to say that you have to say, "Yes" to every request made of you. It is to say that a habit of focusing on the big prize to the exclusion of the little treasures will lead to a place you don't want to live. If the pressures of work or responsibilities are clouding the truly important things in your life, then it's time to stop and take a hard look at where you are headed.

I was fortunate enough to get to see a Disney special the other night that crystallized this lesson for me. The crux of the thread that caught my attention was the father who was a doctor and rarely home. His daughter was assigned to make a documentary on her family, but when the documentary was finished, the father was not in any of the scenes. When he asked her about it, she said that she had gotten tape of him, but she didn't want to embarrass him by showing the scenes that he was in.

He was incredulous and demanded to see the footage. Because I had turned on the show midway through, I hadn't seen how the father had acted when he was around. The scenes were a slap in the face to him and to me. As his kids ran around his office playing tag, he yelled, "Hey! Stop it! Get out of here! Can't you see I'm on the phone?" "One peaceful night to relax! Why is that so much to ask?" "No, I can't do that right now. I have to go to work." "I don't have time. Can't you see I'm busy?"

By the end of the tape, he couldn't watch, and it was hard for me to watch too. Day-to-day it's so easy to get caught up in the big things—those things we think we have to get done. True, they are urgent. But it's worth also asking the question, "Are they important too?"

I believe that in the end when we stand before the throne of Grace and Goodness, God will give a fleeting glance to all those big achievements we've accomplished. However, what He will really take into account is how we treated all those little opportunities that come our way every single day. The opportunity to play with our children while they are young. The opportunity to call a friend we haven't talked to in awhile. The opportunity to share a real piece of our loving nature with someone in need. The opportunity to say, "I'm truly sorry" when we have let someone down.

That is the basis on which we'll be judged. Urgent or important? Big or little? Which are you focused on? (2003)

Getting a New Computer

We know from the Bible that when Jesus comes into our lives, we become a new person in Christ. But do we really understand this concept? Recently I was trying to explain it to a friend of mine, and this friend kept coming back with fear. "I don't want to lose myself." When we finally began to break through what was really going on, he began to accept that there were in fact things that needed to be reassessed and maybe let go of altogether. However, he said, "There were still parts of myself I really liked. I don't want to have to start over."

That's when I came up with how learning to be in Christ is like getting a new computer. Let's say that you have a computer, and it's pretty old. It doesn't work very well anymore. It's slow and not very powerful. But it's comfortable. If you have a computer, you know what I mean. You know where the right icons are to do what you need to do; you know where the files are saved and how; and you know the quirks of this particular computer. So even though it's slow and not very powerful, even though it would be nice to have a new computer, even if this one won't run all the programs you would like, a couple things hold you back.

First, a new computer is expensive. Do you really want to invest the time and money it's going to take to get a new one? Do you want to expend all that effort? Worse, what if you don't like the new one? What if the old one is, in fact, just fine?

So you sit on a computer that is out-dated but comfortable.

Then horror of horrors, the old computer starts giving more problems. Maybe it slows down even further due to a new program or download. Maybe it crashes a couple times, or comes close. Finally, you break down to the point that even getting the new one sounds preferable to dealing with this one. "Okay! Okay! I get it.

Something's gotta change."

So you take the plunge and get a new computer. The first time you plug the thing in and turn it on, the speed is stunning. A blink and it's up. "Wow," you think, "maybe this won't be so bad."

But there comes a time when you have to deal with what's on your old computer and getting the files you really need to the new computer. You start sorting. "This file I need." "This one is completely out-dated." "That one I haven't looked at in 5 years." "This program is one I use all the time." "That one never worked the way I wanted it to, so I won't transfer it."

That's what we do when we get a new life in Christ. We get the opportunity to "go through our files." Does the anger you've held onto make sense to transfer, or is it time to move on to a new way of handling things? How about the joy you are finding in Christ—does it get transferred? Your reliance on yourself? That's one that never worked quite right anyway.

One thing you have to do is *go through the files and decide what you take and what you leave.* Of course, we don't want to do that. We don't want to look at our patterns, our worries, our fears and the other emotions that hold us back. We don't want to deal with those things that have slowed us down and made our hard drives not nearly as efficient as they could be. But in this process, it's important to look through the files we've been running because if we transfer files and programs that don't support who we are now, we slow this new computer down simply because the old programs aren't compatible with the new system.

Since this metaphor came through me, I have realized that I get a new "computer" about every three months or so. I learn, I grow, I get a little more understanding of God, and lo and behold, my new computer won't even run more and more of those unproductive, destructive, old programs anymore!

Fear? I recognize that now, and so on the new computer, I downloaded a virus blocker for it. The new virus blocker is called Faith. Faith immediately alerts me when Fear is trying to get into my computer to cause trouble, and Faith gives me a way to clean Fear off my computer before it does any permanent damage.

Anger? With my Faith Virus Blocker, I got the optional add-on Forgiveness. (I highly recommend this one.) It doesn't delete the anger automatically, but it does allow me to pull up a list of the anger I'm holding, and it gives me the option to permanently delete each occurrence of anger from the hard drive.

Hurt? As a special extra bonus with my Forgiveness add-on, Christ threw in Peace of Mind. The more I use that one, the more I can see other person hurt me out of their own hurt, and what a difference that has made in how my new computer works. Peace of Mind stops me from simply returning the Hurt virus with my hurt. It gives me the option of "Do you want to learn to love like Christ?" Yes or No. What an awesome bonus!

Sorrow? Oh, sorrow. It used to bog my computer down so badly. I was sorry (read: guilty) for everything. If the dishes weren't done, I was sorry. If the dishes were done but the floor hadn't been vacuumed, I was sorry. There was always something to be sorry for. Sorry I had done something and sorry that I hadn't. Everything was filtered through the program called Sorrow.

But along with Faith, Forgiveness, and Peace of Mind, I got the extra, extra special program they were offering. Love. Let me tell you, this is a program to end all programs! It allows me to be gentle with myself. I see now that my old computer filtered all through Sorrow, but Love removes Sorrow altogether. Love has shown me that I did the best I could at the time, and as Love teaches me better, I do better. Love has shown me that the Manufacturer of my computer is not monitoring what I'm doing in order to find something to hold me guilty for. No! In fact, He has implemented a new lifetime warranty that covers all repairs—even if the repair is necessary due to operator negligence and misuse!

I'm so glad for that because to be honest, even with the new computer, I sometimes find myself doing things I know don't work with the new one. But Love... Oh, Love! That's one of those programs I will definitely take with me to the new computer when it's time to get one.

And finally, in the Faith package, there was a program I had never even heard of before. It's called Hope. Hope is a neat little program because as soon as one of the others shows a glitch, as soon as I hit a wrong button, or do something that doesn't compute on this new model, Hope shows me that there is a way to fix it. Before I tried and tried and tried to fix it myself and (let's get wholly honest here!), I only made it worse. With Hope, I now have a direct line to the Manufacturer. I simply dial: Pray & Be Thankful, and it's amazing how fast the issue is resolved.

If you are thinking about getting a new computer because your old one isn't working like you want it to, I highly recommend going with one from the Original Manufacturer. The warranty is the best ever created, the services department is like none other that you've ever dealt with, but best of all, that Faith package will have you asking, "What in the world took me so long to get this new computer? It's absolutely fabulous!" (2006)

Forever

There are some people in the Christian community who believe that only spiritual books, music, and movies can give inspiration of a Godly nature. I am not one of those people. Give me words that speak to my heart and whatever genre they happen to come from, I recognize them as God-imparted.

Therefore, my spiritual quests sometimes don't look very spiritual. I regularly listen to a variety of music for example. Contemporary Christian, old-style gospel, soft rock, country—they seem to run in cycles through my life. And often the non-Christian music, or maybe more specifically, the music that was written to be released not just to Christians often speak to me in ways that are more subtle but just as profound as those stamped "Christian."

A recent example of this in my life has been the music of Keith Urban. Now there are a lot of things I like about his music, starting with the mesmerizing way he can play a guitar. His life too is inspiring to me. He obviously had a God-given dream as well as God-given talent, but while he focused on himself, his life went downhill. When he finally realized how far out of control he was, he made a radical change in his life and reoriented his focus.

That change is evident in his music. Not because he changed genres, but because of the way he now writes the songs that he sings.

Take, for example, one of my favorite parts from his most recent hit, "Days Go By". It goes like this:

"We think about tomorrow then it slips away.
We talk about forever, but we've only got today."

Great advice and insights from a "secular" music maker. How many times do we as Christians put off loving on Tuesday because it's not Sunday? It's as if we have only a limited amount of love, and we don't want to use it up too quickly.

We have great intentions of what we will do tomorrow to help, or next week to give, or next year to be. And while we plan for tomorrow, we miss the chance to help, to give, and to be right now.

So don't think about tomorrow as today slips away. Use today, right now. This minute, and forever will take care of itself.

As the end of "Days Go By" says about our days,

"Take 'em by the hand, yours and mine.
Take 'em by the hand and live your life
Take 'em by the hand, don't let 'em all fly by."

If your focus is on tomorrow, your chances to help, to love, to give will fly by. Live right now. Love right now. Help right now. Give right now, and your forever will take care of itself. (2005)

Expendable

God did not make Hell. Satan did. Like us, Satan was created to be creative, and he certainly is that. God is love. God is open and loving. God never had in mind anything but love. However, Satan decided that love was not enough. It was not enough to be in heaven with God. He wanted more, and he was going to get more. He wanted to be the ruler of his own world. He wanted to be in control. He wanted to be the Prince of something even if that something was Darkness. That way everyone would know how powerful he is.

I've always said that real cool doesn't have to try to be cool, nor does it have to convince anybody that it is cool. Cool is just cool. That's God. He just is. He doesn't have to "try" to be awesome. He just is awesome, and that drives Satan completely crazy with jealousy.

So Satan's goal is to convince us that God wants nothing more than to throw us into the pit of fire forever because we haven't lived up to God's expectations of us. This of course is ridiculous. God loves us so much He sent His only Son to suffer the pain of our sins in our place so that we could live with Him for eternity. I don't know about you, but I can't think of a better example of love. And yet, Satan would like nothing more than to convince us that God's sword of wrath and justice are hanging over our heads every moment as He waits for us to make a mistake, so He can gleefully banish us forever.

The truth is that's Satan's M.O. not God's. Just like so many other things that Satan tells us, this is a lie. You see, where God is love; Satan is leering jealousy and malevolence. He doesn't only want to see us fall, he wants to see us fall hard. The harder we fall, the more pleasure he takes in it. Our downfall is his warped idea of victory. And as it is with Satan, so it is with the world.

If you let it and you don't know this secret, the world will build you up, make you believe it loves you just so it's more fun to watch you fall. One of the most deeply held secrets of Satan is that he believes we are all expendable. At this moment we may be on top of the world. We may be at the top of the ladder, but the reality is that in some tomorrow to come, it will be gone for us, and Satan will not bat an eyelash as we dissolve into tears of disappointment, defeat, and despair because the world no longer assures us that we're great or that we're even needed any more.

Look around. You can see it in the downsizing phenomenon and the outsourcing trends. Workers are no longer people. They are numbers, and when the numbers don't add up, you're gone. There are those who will tell you that as they get older, it is more difficult to keep the job they've had. Why? Because to the world, they are expendable. When they get too old, it is time to move on to someone with more years of usefulness to exploit.

In our culture today, everyone seems to be expendable. Husbands. Wives. Families. Children. Workers. Bosses. Even friends. Notice the divorce rate, the growing number of broken homes, the anxiety over job security. If you fail, if you are ever seen to be human, you are at risk because to the world, you are expendable.

Oh, it's true that the world will act like it likes you when you are "hot." Like when you land that incredible job with the big, fat pay raise. The world will court you like a smitten suitor. It will act like you are the most wonderful thing ever to occupy space under the ozone layer until the moment you are no longer useful, and then it will be as if it never so much as heard of your name.

Years ago, I taught high school for three years. During that time I did my level best to give everything to the school. I showed up early. I went home late. I taught six different classes, ran the newspaper and the yearbook, helped with student council, and the drama club. When I discussed my departure with the principal due to pregnancy, she said she hated to see me go and that she wished I could stay. She didn't know how she could ever replace me.

I had done a lot for that school One of the things I did was update the senior plaques for the two years prior to my arrival and the three years I was there. The next year I walked into that hallway again, and you know what? Life went on without me. There was a new plaque of the new seniors—one that had been done without me. Four years later only two of the office staff even remembered who I was. That's not bad. It's just the way it is.

To the world, you are expendable, but to God you are simply irreplaceable. He wants us with Him more than anything in the world. He loves us beyond all telling. And yet, we spend all our time striving to convince the world that we are what they need, that we are worth their love, that our place can never be taken by anybody else. We twist ourselves into pretzels trying to make them love us when the reality is—they will NEVER love us. The love of the world is hollow. And the world knows that truth better than you do. The world knows you are expendable. More than that, the world believes you are expendable. To them, you are.

So the question becomes are you spending your time fighting to make the world love you, or are you using your time to get better acquainted with the One who already loves you? It's worth considering. (2005)

Drowning Lessons

Any lifeguard will tell you the worst thing that someone the lifeguard is trying to save can do is to "help." A drowning person in a panicked attempt to "save" themselves by thrashing about can end up taking the lifeguard down with them. It's a lesson all of us need to learn no matter how good we are at swimming in spiritual waters.

Many people ask: "What is my purpose here on earth?" They go through various exercises and workshops to find out what their purpose is. I will save you some time and money if you, too, are asking this age-old question.

You have one purpose here on earth, and it can be summed up in two words: to learn.

You were sent here to learn—to learn about yourself—your capabilities, your liabilities, your strengths, your weaknesses, your abilities, and your limitations. You were also sent here to learn about and how to deal with others—those who are easy to love and those for whom God's mercy will have to be super-abundant for their forgiveness to be obtained.

Nonetheless, you were mostly sent here to learn about God and His unending, unfathomable, unstoppable, overwhelming, unbelievable love for you.

One of the biggest lessons and one of the hardest to take and accept is what has been called a disruptive moment. These are the times in your life when you have been easily walking next to the water when suddenly something pushes you in to the deep end.

This something might be someone. It might be an event or an illness or death or a sudden change that blows gaping holes in your belief that all is right with your world.

Suddenly you are buffeted—slapped on every side with wave after wave of despair, doubt, anger, hopelessness, helplessness, grief, anxiety, and fear so strong it pulls you under like a rip tide.

I believe what we are sent here to learn is that it is precisely in these times of trial and fear that we learn the real depth of God. It is in these moments that the Almighty Lifeguard takes hold of us, rather than us holding onto Him.

The problem here is that many of us continue to struggle. We continue to try to save ourselves even as the waves wash over us time and again. What God says to us at these moments is exactly what the lifeguard would say to the drowning person. "Relax. Let Me do it. Do not rely on your strength, trust in Mine."

Your purpose here is primarily to learn that one lesson as deeply as possible. When the storms blow, quit struggling. Trust the Lifeguard.

He has the strength you need. Relax, and let Him work in your life, and you will surely see wonders come from the moments you thought you were destined to drown. By your own effort, you would have. In His strength, however, you will be brought out of the waters of chaos and confusion into a new life you can only know when you have felt both the rip tide and His marvelous, sustaining strength.

In your weakness, His strength can be made manifest. Trust it for it will save you—especially when you feel you are drowning. (2006)

C+ Moments

Okay, let's get real. We've all had them. Those horrible, horrendous, completely awful moments in life when we did our best, but when we get the report card back, it's not the grade we hoped it would be. My daughter recently had such a moment. It had been an extraordinarily tough semester, and during the last six weeks, the wheels came off the wagon.

She was stressed. Too much homework. Too much reading. Way too much math. Too little sleep. No time to play. No time to draw or climb or just be. And she's only in the fourth grade.

Then came the report card with the C+ in Social Studies. I understood the reality that at her school a C+ is an 84, and an 84 is not failing in anybody's book. However, the C+ did mean that she fell off of the A-B honor roll she'd been on since early in her third grade year (they don't give letter grades before that). So here she was on the downside of the grading curve with the last grade tallied, and it wasn't what she'd hoped it would be.

My C+ moment came when I was in the fifth grade—only mine was a B+, and I cried for a week. Up to then, I had been an A student. A honor roll every six weeks from first grade on. Then I hit the solid brick wall of "I should've done more." Having learned a few lessons about the grade not being YOU from my experience, I knew I had to find a way to turn my daughter's C+ into a blessing though clearly in disguise.

I told her that the C+ simply meant we had to work harder the next six weeks, that I would take a more active roll in helping her, and that I was proud of her for doing her best in a tough situation. During the next six weeks, she learned that it was all right to ask if she didn't know something. She learned to overcome her penchant for getting distracted by using CD's of relaxing water. She learned to concentrate on math and to not take on so much for reading. By the time the report cards came out the next semester, I knew she was doing better.

I didn't know how much better until she opened it and started calling out the grades to me. A. A. A... You got it. She made the A honor roll for the first time ever. She took the C+ and made lemonade!

It was a great lesson for her. It was a better lesson for me. How many times do I look at the C+ moments or the F moments of my life—those times when I feel like a complete failure, those times when I struck out so many times it's pointless to keep trying... How many times have I taken those moments and used them as an excuse to quit rather than seeing them as an opportunity to observe what isn't working and change it?

Is that easy? No. She still had to study. She still had to seek answers for better ways to study. But the point is not that it was easy, the point is she was willing to take a C+ moment and turn it into a lesson she can learn from forever. In my books, that deserves an A+. (2006)

Comfort

A word that has recently popped up to be explored is "comfort." Now, if you're like me, you think this word has to do with giving compassion to someone at a weak place in their lives. To an extent that's true, but let's look at what comfort really means and see how much better we understand what we are doing when we give comfort.

The first part of comfort is "com" which means "with." Compassion means "with passion." Comfort therefore means with something. But what?

Here's where the word turned on its head for me. The second part of comfort is... "fort." Fort? What? Doesn't that mean "strength"? If you want to be safe, you go to a fort. Fortitude is one of the Gifts of the Holy Spirit which means strength and courage.

So, comfort means "with strength"? Funny. I'd never thought of strength when thinking of comforting someone. But on closer inspection, that's exactly what we aim to do when giving comfort—to give someone strength, fortitude, courage to endure the suffering they are now faced with.

For some reason this understanding gives new meaning to my efforts to comfort someone in times of crisis. Before I was simply commiserating with them. Now, I realize that I am offering them the strength to persevere in spite of opposition and obstacles. That strength may come through a simple hug, a kind word, or a long conversation. However it comes, it is a piece of strength that will help them face and deal with the current situation.

I don't know about you, but to me, that is an awesome opportunity—far more valuable than I ever previously understood. (2006)

Drowning in Feelings

There are times in this life that all of us get immersed in a swirl of feelings that are ridiculously hard to sort out. They race around the track of our mind, darting in and out of our consciousness, making us feel out-of-whack and lacking control.

Maybe the precipitating cause was something done to us. Maybe it is something that was done to someone we love. Maybe it's a world event that shakes our inmost calm. Sorting it all out seems impossible because there are so many differing feelings, so many divergent paths.

There is a way to sort them out. It doesn't take long. And all it requires is a pen and paper. This is equally effective for new issues and problems that have plagued you for years.

Here are the four basic statements. Write each as many times as necessary filling in the end with as many things as you can think of for the specific situation you are wanting to work through.

I am angry because…
I am sad/hurt because…
I am afraid that…
I am sorry for…

As you write each, let the feelings come up with them. Write them, and get them out so they will no longer be on loop in your brain and your body.

When you finish those four, then write out the following statement several times for each person involved in this situation (including yourself).

I forgive _____, and I release him/her to the love and gentleness of the Holy Spirit.

When you have finished with the forgiveness statement, there may be a void in your being from all of the feelings you have released. It is important to fill that gap with something positive.

So, next write as many endings for each of these statements that you can think of.

I am grateful for/that…
I give thanks to God for…
My life is great because…

Do this two or three times over the course of a week and the negative, soul-sapping feelings you are experiencing should begin to subside as new creative ways to handle the situation emerge. (2007)

Called

Twice in the last week I got called. The first was by a lady whose children are the same age as mine. This lady is someone I've admired for many years. The purpose of her call was to see if I would run for the school board of my daughters' school.

She told me the qualifications, described the job, and told me why they thought I would be good for the position. It was a very thorough offer. I listened to her, and then I listened to my heart. Make no mistake, it was flattering to be wanted. It felt good that someone would think of me for such a position. However, as I took serious stock of where I am right now and what the Holy Spirit has laid on my heart, I knew the only answer I could give her was, "No."

Two days later I got a second call. This one came from a long-time friend of mine. Although she and I had previously discussed the reason for her call, and although I had already declined at least twice, she was calling again. The offer? To join one of the women's organizations at our church.

When I said, "No, but thanks," she couldn't understand why. After all, it's only one night a month, the circle is women my own age, it's a reason to get out of the house, you can serve your community, they are really nice, and it's fun. (If I missed any of the reasons she gave me, I apologize.) Even after all of her reasons, I still said, "No." And to be honest, I still don't think she understands.

Now, please hear me loud and clear—there is nothing wrong with either of these organizations. In fact, they do a lot of great work for the community and for the church. The school board is certainly a worthwhile way to give of yourself, and women's organizations do a lot of good work in our world.

However, when I looked in my heart at this time in my life—with young children, a husband who often works out of town, and the writing ministry that God has shown me time and again He wants me to do—I simply do not feel called to the other organizations. Could I do them? Yes. Could I do them well? Yes. But in my heart I know they would be taking time away from what He really has called me to do.

There may well come a time when I do feel called to these again. After all, it wouldn't be the first time I helped out. In high school, I was an usher at church, I played guitar and sang in three choirs, I was the vice president of the youth organization, and I read in church. In short, I was involved.

On the other hand, right now, I have three children whom I shall never get this time to spend with them back. To be sure, I already miss too much time with them. It's a balance I don't always hold so well. But when I looked at these offers, and put them on the scales with their importance versus what I feel as God's call for this time in my life—namely raising my children and my writing, the children and writing won out.

Right now, I am called to be here for them, to be able to drop everything if need be if they need me. If I am tied to meetings and service projects, that would not be possible.

Is everyone called to that? No, probably not. It takes getting still long enough to listen to the whisper of the Holy Spirit in your heart to decide. When you take the time to do that, the real call will be clear—whether the phone actually rings or not. (2005)

Close Your Eyes, Say a Prayer, and Kick It

I truly love how many life-changing lessons from God are brought home in the simplest of situations. Recently one such situation was related to me from my younger sister. Her son is playing soccer for the first time this year. Being a natural athlete, he took to this sport with his usual grace and ease. Apparently the whole team has gelled well. Going into the game that night they were undefeated.

The problem was, so was the other team. It was a battle of defenses the whole night. In short, regulation time expired with a 0-0 tie. Now in soccer, ties are decided on sudden death kicks. At this level each player on each team gets a free kick. After one team goes, the other goes until the tie is broken.

My nephew was chosen goalie for the overtime period. All five of the other team lined up, and one by one, they took a shot at the goal. One by one, my nephew stopped the balls until all had tried, and the score was still 0-0.

After a trip to the opposite goal, my nephew's teammates each took a shot. Nine team members took a free kick, but not a single one went in. Last to go, my nephew stepped up to take his kick. He closed his eyes, took a breath, and with quiet determination sent the ball flying into the upper left corner for the only goal of the game.

As she recounted the story, my sister said, "I wish every parent on earth had the opportunity to watch their child just once make the winning goal. He was jumping around the field. He was so excited. It was awesome!"

Then she related the rest of the story—you know the part that was going on but that you couldn't see from your seat in the stands. My sister asked her son after the game, "So, were you nervous standing out there waiting for your turn?"

He said, "No. I just stood there and prayed while the other ones kicked."

Very cool answer. But wait! It gets better.

My brother-in-law, ever the one to plan and strategize asked, "So, were you trying to make it in the goal right there at the top?"

You've got to love the answer my beautiful nephew gave. "No, not really. I just closed my eyes, said a prayer, and kicked it."

Such profound wisdom from one so young. How often do we stand on the field of our dreams—paralyzed by the thought that we might miss this shot and lose it for the whole team? How often do we analyze, twistize, and strategize ourselves into pretzels trying to figure out the best way to do it, what we can do to win the game, and what happens if we don't win?

But here's a great secret. If you are on God's team, it's not up to you anyway. Just close your eyes, say a prayer, and kick it. Do your best, and then put it in His hands. Trust me on this, if you do that, you will win far more games and get to jump all over that field in victory as your Heavenly Father looks on with pride, joy, and excitement as He watches the child that He loves so very, very much celebrate the great victory of a life well-lived. (2006)

5

On Writing

He wants not only us but everyone saved, you know, everyone to get to know the truth we've learned: that there's one God and only one, and one Priest-Mediator between God and us— Jesus, who offered himself in exchange for everyone held captive by sin, to set them all free. This and only this has been my appointed work, getting this news out to those who have never heard of God, and explaining how it works by simple faith and plain truth. (1 Timothy 2:4-7 TMB)

Prolific

Prolific. It's a funny word to be sure. Many people have said that about me—I'm a prolific writer. I know what it means. They think I write a lot, and I do, I guess. Compared with most people you meet, I do write a lot. However, I don't feel like I write that much. In fact, I wish I could write more.

To me, writing is a time I can open myself to be amazed at what God says through me. Stream of consciousness and all that. It is capturing His thoughts, His insights that is so enthralling.

I do not aim to be more prolific as a writer so much as I long to be more prolific as a listener and a transcriber of His glory in my life.

If that makes me prolific, then, yes, I guess I am. (2006)

A Different Idea

As I sat in the chapel on that sunny Thursday evening, I was under the impression things were going pretty well. The music for the weekend was ready, my speech had finally been accepted, and my books were to be handed out to everyone there—or so I thought.

Then the news: "We will not be handing out your books. We only want those here to think about God." Okay, granted she'd never actually read the book in question. She didn't know it was about forgiveness and letting God into your life.

Logic said I should be hurt and angry. The world's logic said I should argue with her, explain the book, make her understand so she would agree to hand them out. However, I didn't. I just sat there nodding, "Okay. Okay."

Two days later after my speech, a Holy Spirit friend and I walked into my room. Now this particular Holy Spirit friend was one of my readers from when I first started writing. In fact, she is arguably my most ardent fan. She knew I had donated the books, but she didn't know about the Thursday conversation because I hadn't told anyone.

"Oh, they brought the books back," I said, seeing the three boxes stacked on the desk.

"Back?" she asked in horror. "Why didn't they hand them out?"

So I told her they had decided not to hand them out. She got really quiet and said, "May I ask why?"

I told her what they told me, and then I said, "But that's okay. It just means the Holy Spirit has a different idea."

"Yeah, but they haven't even read it. They didn't even give it a chance. How can they say it's not enough about God if they haven't even read it?"

From the world's perspective that argument made perfect sense.

However, what I have learned is that concentrating on the disappointments the world tries to convince you are horribly hurtful prevents you from opening your spirit to the blessings the Holy Spirit is wanting to send your way. To the world it looks like an unfair setback, but to me, it just means the Holy Spirit has a different idea.

Sure enough, He cleared the way for me to make the books available to some friends who then handed them out to friends I had never even met—some who were there, some who were not. All were exactly who the Holy Spirit wanted to get them the whole time.

It wasn't a disappointment—the Holy Spirit just had a different idea. (2005)

34 Lives

Don't freak out. It's not what you think, but I have to this point on earth lived 34 lives. Let me explain. In general, there are two ways to write a novel. The first way is to plot everything, to research, outline and plan every plot twist and event from page one to the final page before you ever write the first word. The other way is sometimes called Seat of the Pants—meaning you don't know much about the story, you just start writing and let the book come to life as you write.

I use a lot of both ways, but I tend to think of it as doing what the Holy Spirit wants when He wants it done. Most of the time I start knowing at least a scene or two of what happens. Sometimes all I know is who the characters are, sometimes I know bits and pieces of the story. No matter how they start, each and every story has stretched me and forced me to grow in its own way. I see the stories as Holy Spirit lessons in many ways.

The first way is I've learned I have to let go of "how I did it last time." However I did it last time is never how I will do it this time— that much I have learned. This time will always be different. This time will always have it's own lesson to teach me.

The second way these stories have taught me is to give me the chance to live many lives—not just this experience I myself call life. In some ways my characters are pieces of me. In some ways I'm pieces of them. When I write, for that time I "become" them. I often take on various characteristics of them as I'm writing their story. I've dressed new age for a time because that's how one character often dressed. I've worn leather wristbands because that's what a character wore. When I'm in character mode, I listen to the world in a different way. I listen the way they would.

I listen for the lessons they need to learn in the way they need to learn it, and in the process, I learn. It's a cool way to learn because as heart wrenching as a circumstance in a book is, I have the option of turning off the computer and processing for awhile. In real life, you can't do that.

Through my characters I have experienced poverty and riches far beyond what I will ever have. I have worried about where my next meal will come from and about how to save a youth center from being closed. I have jumped off the edge of sanity into alcohol and relived a drug addiction. I have seen the loneliness of getting the dream you thought you wanted but missing the things that are truly important along the way. And with every experience, I have learned in a way I couldn't have from my own experience.

To date I have completed 17 novels. Since I write from the point of view of the hero and that of the heroine in each book, I have now lived 34 lives. This unique life experience—both my life and getting to marinate in others' souls for a time—has taught me many things about this life that I couldn't have learned had I only lived my own life experience.

I firmly believe that being able to walk in each of my characters' shoes for a time has given me knowledge that I would not have otherwise been privy to gaining in any other way. It has opened my eyes to how a single situation can be interpreted in radically different ways depending on the particular perspective of an individual involved. Because of this, I now understand that no matter how firmly you believe your experience is definitive, the other person is probably as adamant that their interpretation is the only valid one as well.

This knowledge has saved me on more than one occasion from assuming that because my interpretation of events was X that everyone else's was too. I am more willing to listen to other perspectives. I am more willing to dig for what's really going on rather than assuming I know and going on faulty personal interpretation.

It's a lesson I greatly value, and one I will forever be glad that God allowed me to have. How else could you live 34 lives and not be counted insane? Unless of course you were to read other's experiences... hmm.... There's an idea. (2005)

Romance and God:
The Connection

And the Lord said, "it is not good for the man to be alone; I will make him a helper comparable to him." --Genesis 2:18

Time and again since I've started writing Inspirational Romance, I've encountered the question, "What does God have to do with romance?" To which, I respond with amazement, "Everything!" To me, one of the most sacred mysteries is the love between a man and a woman, how two distinct lives can be cleaved together and become one forever. It is fascinating. It is the basis of all of life. Yet I think it is one of the most misunderstood elements of our society today.

The confusion begins when we do not appreciate the difference between the body and the spirit. The body is limited. Asked to touch the ceiling without a ladder or a chair, and you might be hard-pressed to figure out how to do that. The spirit, on the other hand, is unlimited. Lie on the grass and let your spirit soar with a kite high into a soft blue sky, and it will have no problem doing that. This is the first roadblock that society has put up between God and romance. Society says that romance is based on bodies—the physical. God says romance is based in the spirit.

Be completely humble and gentle; be patient, bearing with one another in love. Make every effort to keep the unity of the Spirit through the bond of peace. —Ephesians 4:2-3

How but in God can two souls touch, fall in love, and be bonded together forever? How but in God can a couple weather the crises that inevitably come in marriage? How but with God at the center of the household can man and wife become one flesh until death do them part? How, indeed?

But the messages promoted by society say that to find a spouse, you must first twist yourself and your beliefs into unrecognizable patterns to make yourself "attractive" to another. To be attractive you must focus almost exclusively on the physical, ignore the spiritual, and forget God until you're ready to get married. From this point-of-view, it's no wonder that people think romance and God are exclusive clubs, and you cannot belong to both.

To me, that's sad because God meant the mystery of marriage to be the most intimate relationship two people can have. True intimacy is romantic in itself, and true intimacy is based not on the physical but on the spiritual connection that two people share, the connection that God Himself ordained as holy.

Let marriage be held in honor among all. —Hebrews 13:4

And this connection starts when the couple first meets—not at the altar.

By divorcing God from romance, we have taken God out of the relationship between man and woman. So instead of explaining that in God and through God, your relationship can be based on something real, and holy, and lasting, we throw our sons and daughters to the winds. Telling them either, "Sex is bad. It is a sin." Or we give them condoms in schools on the erroneous belief that "kids will be kids." To me, both are cop-outs. We need to guide our kids (and inform ourselves) that if God is at the center of the relationship from the beginning, sex before marriage shouldn't even be a question.

Why? Because true love is about getting to know one another on a deeper level than physical, because when you find true love, you want what is best for the other person, and because sex-before-marriage is always based on fear rather than love. If it is love, if this relationship is forever in the eyes of God, why not get married first? Reality is, marriage solidifies the union in the eyes of society, in God's eyes, and in the eyes of the participants. Therefore, if it's true love, why not wait? Waiting is respectful to both partners. It will strengthen the commitment. It will solidify trust. And it holds to the belief that God is indeed the center of this union, and He will make a time and a place for everything.

God and romance? In the same breath? What a radical concept, but so overwhelmingly wonderful when it becomes the center of your relationship with another.

For love is from God and everyone that loves is born of God and knows God...for God is love. --1 John 4:7-8

It's a standard we should all strive for.

(2002)

And the Greatest of These is Love

All writers know the faith it takes to put words on paper. They've seen the faith required to search for the right word, the right nugget of truth that will mark their work as top-notch. Ultimately, they know the gut-wrenching faith it takes to turn their written baby over to someone who might reject it outright.

They know hope too. Even after they've been kicked to the curb by an agent who probably didn't even read the first sentence of a query, after a few days of chocolate and Kleenexes, hope surges again. Maybe the next editor will love it, buy it, publish it, and send it into the world to be included next to John Grisham's on the front table of every bookstore in the country. Don't deny it. If you write, you know that hope is real.

One element, however, sometimes gets lost when faith and hope begin to emerge in our writing journey. That element is love. Sure, we love it, or we wouldn't stress ourselves out to learn how to do it better, to find someone to publish it, and to put ourselves on the chopping block of rejection time and again. It's almost a given that we love it. The problem is we forget that we love it.

As a character who loves music in one of my books says, "You know me, I'd play for the squirrels if they'd listen."

Too often the longer we write, the less we remember what we love about it. Our focus shifts from writing for love to writing so others will love what we've written.

When we write for the love of it, every frustrating moment is an exhilarating challenge. Shaping the ephemerally picturesque stories in our minds into something coherent and fluid is like no other experience. The very act of putting that last piece of our word puzzle into place has no equal.

Remember the journals you kept, the poems you wrote, the

short stories that are still tucked away in some old notebook. You wrote those not to gain love but because they were burning a hole in your soul to be put on paper.

Then you began writing not for love but to gain love. You became convinced that you had to twist your writing to meet what others believe is marketable or publishable. And so you let your love for writing morph into wanting your writing to be loved... sometimes at all costs. You twisted yourself into a pretzel, learning perfect grammar, point of view, the "correct" way to write a marketable manuscript.

Learning and growing in your writing is one thing, but when that gets so tangled in the rules that you forget why you started in the first place, that is something altogether different. Love is the key to writing real. As the Bible says so eloquently:

In the end three things shall last, faith, hope, and love. And the greatest of these is love. –1 Corinthians 13:13

It's a lesson every writer should take to heart. (2005)

6

On God as Life

So let God work His will in you. *(James 4:7, TMB)*

Plugging Into the Source

How do you live a life of peace, hope, joy, and love? Well, you can take the option of trying to get these by what the world says brings them. You can get married to Mr. or Ms. Right. You can work yourself silly and earn a million bucks. You can earn several degrees. Or you could pack it all in and travel to some remote island to get away from it all.

The problem with each of these ways is they just don't work. Take the marriage part. If you are single, it's highly likely that you have the thought that "If I was just married, then I would be happy." However, may I direct your attention now to the over 50% divorce rate in this country? It's pretty clear that marriage alone will not automatically make you happy.

Well, then what about money? Isn't the acquisition of great wealth an indicator of overall happiness? It could be except for one thing: How much is great wealth? Is it something in savings? Is it $100,000? Is it a million? Two? Four? Ten?

The problem with the idea that wealth accumulation on its own will bring happiness is that whatever level you are at, you can still feel miserable. And then it's logical to think, "Well, if I only had a little more." In fact, J.D. Rockefeller, the great tycoon, said just that when asked what constituted great wealth. So money in and of itself is not that answer.

How about all those degrees? I know people who have been in perpetual college for years, and they are not happy. Some are too scared to get out and get a job. Some believe that with the "next" degree they will finally feel worth something. So they pursue and pursue and pursue, and sadly never attain the feeling they are working so hard to gain.

Okay, so those don't work. What about that island? There's an old saying, "Wherever you go, there you are." And therein lies our main problem. It is not that any of those outside things are bad. Finding the love of your life is great—as long as you're ready to be great in the relationship. There are lots of great things you can do with money, provided you are at a place in your head and heart to be able to do them. Learning and education are essential in our society, but they can do nothing if not put to good use. And vacations are nice, but you're still you on vacation, and you're still you when you get back.

So what's the answer to finding peace? The answer is plugging into the Source of all that is. I told a friend of mine recently to start "installing outlets." An outlet is simply a way to get in touch with God. Outlets can be many things, and they will be different for each person.

Here are some off the top of my head…

Reading, writing, listening to music, listening to lectures on becoming who you are meant to be, going to church, reading the Bible, praying, holding or playing with a child, having a pet, enjoying this moment (whatever it happens to be), doing something you love that's creative—painting, building, swimming, running. You can do meditation, spiritual retreats, and adoration. You can teach Sunday school or sing in the choir.

It's not about your service for Him, it's about installing one more way in your life through which He can talk to you. Plugging into Him is deceptively easy once you do it. Once you live there, you will know when you are not plugged in, and you will instinctively find ways to plug in again because you have learned that being plugged in is where the juice of life is found.

So evaluate your spiritual house. How many outlets do you have to receive His power? Is there only one behind the bed that is really hard to reach, or are they everywhere you look? And as you are installing these outlets, be sure to get quiet and ask if this particular outlet will lead YOU to peace. Just because someone else's outlet works for them, it doesn't mean it will work for YOU.

You install YOUR outlets and begin to let God's power work through you, and I guarantee you, there will be other "houses" coming up saying, "Hey, whatever you've got, I want some too!" (2006)

Life Value

Everyone understands that if you sell something, you get a cash return. This return may be large or small depending on the quality of the product or service. The cash value of any particular item may be expressed in dollars and cents. A widget may cost $5.00 or a super-widget may cost $5,000.

What most people don't understand, however, is the concept of "life value." In other words the value in enhanced life-terms that the purchaser gains in return for trading their cash for a product or service. Recently when I read about this concept, I went, "Wow! I'd never thought of it like that." What I was particularly impressed with was how different this makes life itself feel as it is expressed through me and as I look at others.

A simple example (and the one I am most familiar with) is brought to expression in my books. My first collection of short stories "Reflections On Life" was recently published. The cash value of this book is $12.95. In order to purchase the book, that is what a reader would have to pay for it. However, the life value can vary widely depending on the purchaser.

Let's say I talked someone who never reads into purchasing "Reflections." This person would turn over $12.95, take the book home, put it on their shelf, and the life value of that book would be zero—unless by some miraculous intervention it fell into the hands of another person who was a reader.

Now, let's take that same book. The cash value is still $12.95; however, this time the purchaser is not only an avid reader but fully engaged in learning about life and putting that knowledge into action. In this instance, the life value may well be immeasurable because that person will take the concepts in the book, apply them to their lives and the lives of those around them, and life increases for everyone involved—whether the other people directly read the book or not.

As I thought about this concept, I realized how transferable to other circumstances it is. My brother-in-law for instance is a banker. He deals mostly in granting loans to farmers and individuals for homes and cars. If he were to talk someone into taking out a loan that they did not need, the life value of that loan could well be negative because it would drain the borrower's spirit as well as their pocketbook. However, if he lends money to a farmer for instance, and that farmer uses the loan to purchase seed and equipment to grow and harvest the crop that results, the life value of that loan is surely immeasurable. Not only does the farmer make a profit and thereby enhance his life by being able to provide for his own family, but the fruits of his labor enhance the life value of every person who then purchases and consumes or uses the products that results from this crop.

Isn't that an awesome way to think about what you do for a living?

And there are other prime examples in my own family. My mother and my sister both baby sit. The cash value of what they do pales so far in comparison to the life value of that endeavor that it's ridiculous! And another example, my brother sells tools to fix cars. Each tool he sells has the capacity to enhance the life of the mechanic who buys it because he can now do in 2 minutes what would've taken 2 hours to do with the wrong tool. Not only that, but that one tool has enhanced the life of every person whose car it is used to fix. It also enhances the lives of all those other drivers on the road who are now safer because that car is working properly. It also conceivably enhances the lives of those who drive and ride in that car—to work, to school, to Grandma's for Christmas. Think of the life value of that one, simple sale!

My brother's wife has recently begun cleaning houses. Think of the time these families now have to be together enjoying life rather than picking up and vacuuming because of her contribution to their lives. She also gives her time (not paid) to help at her children's schools and their various teams and clubs. There is literally no telling how much life value she is adding to the existence not only of her children but of all of the children who benefit from her efforts. Life value abounds from her efforts!

My husband builds things. He builds houses. He fixes doors. He builds cabinets. Each and every fix-it job and new construction that he lends his hands to increases the life value of someone and sometimes that of many someones. Innumerable people have walked through doors that work because of him. They have stored important information in cabinets he built. They have lived and raised their children in houses that he built. Life. Life. Life in the extreme—not because of cash value but because of life value.

And it gets better. My father is the janitor and the baseball coach for my hometown high school. He spends his days making sure the teachers have what they need to be able to impart knowledge to a whole passel of children. The cash value of this may not be huge, but the life value is astronomical to the point that you cannot even count it!

So the question is: When you think about the value of what you are doing, do you assess your success only in terms of cash value—thereby trying to sell whether the product will enhance or diminish the purchaser's life, or do you make a serious effort to greatly multiply the purchaser's life experience through your product or service? It's a great question, and life looks very different depending on which "value" you are focused on.

The examples are everywhere! Walk down an aisle at the grocery store. Look at a box of cereal or a bottle of medicine. You pay cash value of $3 to $10 for this purchase, but it makes you full or makes you well. Life value.

Once you understand this concept, take a moment to visualize those who have traded hours of their lives to enhance YOUR life value. There's the life value of the person who came up with the grocery cart you are pushing. Think of the time-savings and therefore the life value that represents. There is the person who built the shelves so that the products can be displayed in an orderly fashion.

There is the person who put those shelves together. There is the person who stocked those shelves so you can just walk in and buy what you need without hours of searching. There is the person who created the item that you are buying—the person who came up with the type of cereal, the person who figured out that "this combination of molecules" will cause your body to do this and thus get well.

The reality is that life value is everywhere you look. When you take life value for granted or discount it because you are focused on cash value, you're missing the point completely. Try it. I challenge you. Begin to look at life value for one day, and if it doesn't completely change how you look at life, you can always go back to measuring everything in dollars and cents. (2005)

Life Expressing Itself Through Life

If you read, understand, and put this lesson into practice, you will never look at life the same way. It is completely incredible the profound change in how I look at absolutely everything since this thought went through me. The thought is simple: "Life (God) has designed a world so that He can have the opportunity to express Life (Himself) by living it through us." Read that again. It took me several run-throughs to begin to understand what He was telling me in this statement. Here is another way to say it:

"Life has designed a world in which He has the opportunity to express His Life through living it."

This understanding is the fusion of several different inputs. One being a book by Neale Donald Walsch called, *Communion with God. Communion* delves into the illusions of what we call life—such as failure, superiority, and conditionality. This book talks "about" God's plan for life as if God Himself is talking about life.

The second book is called *The Science of Getting Rich* by Wallace D. Wattles. Although it sounds like this book is about money, that is only one of the physical manifestations of its premise. The premise is basically that we aspire to be more, live more, and experience more because God aspires to be more, live more, and experience more. He has chosen to do that through us. It is Life expressing itself through life.

Hear what I am saying here because it will change everything. It will change how you look at money, at your work, at your life, and at the lives of others. If this concept is true, if Life created life in order to experience more of itself, then as we allow ourselves to live, to create, to enjoy, to laugh, to love, to cry, to learn... we are not just experiencing that for ourselves, we are allowing God Himself to experience those things through us.

Money? We no longer have to grasp for money if we are allowing God to live through us. Why? Because God is Everything, and He will naturally attract everything He needs to live life more fully to Himself and thereby to us. It is no longer a question of us asking, begging, and bargaining with Him for what we want. We fully recognize that our "desires" come from Him. They are "of the Father." They are HIS desire to live more fully not just us wanting something.

To the world, this probably sounds like "grab all the money you can so you can live it up." However, that's not what this is really saying because that mentality/spirituality is death not life. Grabbing everything and hurting others to get it creates destruction and despair, not life and hope. God, however, *is* life and hope; therefore, why would He choose to bring something to Him in a way or for a purpose that is something He is not?

No, when you open your life and let Him live through you, those things He desires are naturally attracted to you. More, in actuality, they are already yours, for your life is now God's life, and God is everything.

This concept will also change how you deal with people because you will recognize the God in them striving to express life. To those who get this, you will be attracted. To those who do not, you may well be given opportunities (think of a simple smile) to turn the way they are currently living to this new paradigm.

It is blazingly simple and yet so profound as to be nearly impossible to grasp. God, right now, wants to experience Life through you, are you letting Him, or are you just existing to serve yourself because some deity somewhere put you here until they take you away? (2005)

Life and Death

Life is God. Death is "not God." When you truly have life, what you have done is to allow God to permeate you so fully that "you" have begun to disappear, and He has begun to live through you. Death is the opposite of this. Death reigns when you are relying on your own power, your own resources, your own strength, your own knowledge and understanding in any given situation.

In the Garden of Eden, there were two trees—the Tree of Life, and the Tree of the Knowledge of Good and Evil. The Tree of Life was quite simply allowing God to live life in and through His creations. The Tree of the Knowledge of Good and Evil was the belief that we don't need God, that we could live and do it on our own. The moment Adam and Eve ate of the Tree of the Knowledge of Good and Evil, death came into the world because they chose to rely on themselves rather than on God.

Instantly, they were banished from the garden, the sanctuary that God had made for them, and they were sent out into the world to learn to fend for themselves literally because that's what they had chosen. However, this truth did not begin and end with this one act. It is going on every day in every life capable of making choices on this planet.

That means you.

Yes, you have the choice between letting God live through you or trying to do it on your own. Which are you choosing? I have come to wonder why God sent Jesus into the world with this concept in mind. I believe the answer to that is very simple. He sent Christ who is a part of Himself into the world to restore our choice to rely on God rather than on ourselves. Once again, through Jesus Christ, we have the choice to choose the Tree of Life rather than having as our only option the Tree of the Knowledge of Good and Evil manifested in the laws laid out as a measure of whether we are good enough to be allowed back into God's grace.

On our own, of course we are not good enough. We can't be, for on our own, we are death—literally. On our own, we have no life within us because if we are doing it on our own, that necessarily means that God is not in us. If God is not in us, Life is not in us and we are dead. For God is Life; death is the absence of Life or stated another way, death is the absence of God.

Living on our own we are told that we must rely on competition for limited resources. We must beat others out for the best education and the means to provide for ourselves because if we don't beat them, they will take some and there will be less for us. When we are living on our own, we do not believe that God is All and Everything and that He will provide. No. Instead we believe that if *we* don't do it, it won't get done. We believe in the empty promises of worldly success and achievement. We seek to impress one another with our wealth, our knowledge, and our worldly attributes—however altruistic they may seem on the outside.

None of this is real. It is death personified, and yet over and over again, we choose this avenue of "being." Even in the Christian life, our service often comes not from God living through us, but from us trying to prove ourselves worthy of Him. It is a fallacy, a lie of the highest proportions. God does not seek our effort. He seeks only to express Himself and His love through us.

It is like Mark Hall from Casting Crowns said when he recounted the story of God making his life's purpose perfectly clear: "Mark, I'm going to do something wonderful in the world. I just want to know if you want to come along."

God seeks to live through us, and when we allow Him to do that, that is Life. That is the Life that Christ came to remind was an option and to make possible once again.

Through His cross, Christ took onto Himself the shame of the children of God who had tried so valiantly to live up to what God wanted them to be and had failed so miserably, and He allowed that fallacy to be nailed to a cross and forever banished. When He arose, Life arose with Him. When He sent His Spirit, He sent it to once again live in us and through us.

And still, we choose death over Him. Why? Good question.

Now you know the truth, is death still your choice? (2005)

Creation or Competition?

This is a concept I've known intuitively for a long, long time. I grew up in a very competitive family that lived in a very competitive town that resided in a very competitive state, which was a part of a very competitive country, which was a small part of a very competitive world. In one way I was not a competitive child because I was not good at sports—any sport in any way. However, I see now how competitive I was in other areas like academics and band. Mostly I didn't compete with others; mostly I competed with myself, and often I lost.

One such competition I remember in the depths of who I am. I was in the fifth grade, and up until that year I had literally made A's in everything. Every subject. Every six weeks since I'd been in the first grade. And then I got that report card with a—gasp—B! I was crushed, devastated, destroyed.

We found out that the B represented the underlying score of 89. 89. One point from an A, and in all likelihood only 10th's of a point away, and yet those 10ths represented a chasm between who I thought I had to be in order to be worth something and who I felt like I now was.

It sounds so silly. How many people get devastated over a B? In fact, I'm sure if you didn't get straight A's all through school, you are probably saying, "Ah, poor baby. You got a B. It's tragic." But understand, to me, it was tragic. It was as if who I thought I was had died. Tears couldn't bring her back. Sorrow and guilt over what I could have or should have done to gain those coveted 10ths of a point couldn't bring the opportunity back. Nothing could.

As this period of my life progressed, my family over and over explained that it was all right. They still loved me. I came to accept that I wasn't perfect and that my worth wasn't my grades, but it was immensely difficult, and in truth it took until I was in college to really believe them.

So I know what havoc living with a competition-mind set can wreak in a life.

Competition has several underpinnings that are present when it is. The first is a belief in separateness. I am separate from those I am competing with, and thus, one of us can be better, smarter, more worthy of praise than the other. Another underpinning belief is that the good things in this life are inherently limited; therefore, if you want some of the good stuff, you must necessarily beat out someone else to get it.

These two lead to the dominant underpinning which is fear. For if I am separate, I am alone, and if I must necessarily fight for the limited resources, my ability must be greater than that of everyone else who is competing, or I will suffer. These equal one thing: Fear.

If I am in competition with you, and you get something I wanted, it follows that I will separate myself further from you, fall into greater fear, and believe more deeply that I must get better to get more. We see the attempt to subvert the naturalness of this progression played out at the end of a game (whatever the game). It's called "sportsmanship." Win or lose, you should shake the opposing squads hands as a sign of respect. But the truth is win or lose, you don't *want* to shake their hand. Why? Because if you've won, this show of respect necessarily brings the loser back up if not up to your level than closer. If you've lost, shaking the winner's hand affirms they are better than you and something you valued has been lost.

The world's dominant teaching is competition. We are taught from early on:

You must "learn to play the game."

You must maximize your ability to win (or get run over if you don't).

You have to do your best.

Study hard.

Work hard.

Play fair.

Make success your goal.

Accomplish. Triumph. Win.

All of these are the aims of a competitive world.

God is not competitive.

Let me repeat that: God is not competitive. God does not have to compete because in the simplest terms, who would He compete against? He who made the universe by saying, "Let there be..." could beat everyone at anything without so much as trying. God's power does not come from being competitive. No. God's power comes from being creative.

God creates. That's what He does. If He wants a mountain, He creates a mountain. He doesn't go out and try to talk someone else out of their mountain, nor does He work to gain a piece of a mountain. He doesn't have to. He can simply create a mountain, and so in a sense can we.

I have a young friend who wanted a laptop computer. She pined for one, begged for one, was desperate to get one. At the time she was learning to play the piano, and was early enough in her piano experience that competition hadn't entered the scene yet. One evening I told her mother to tell her that instead of "competing" for the laptop, she should concentrate on creating with her music. The more you create, the more "things" will flow to you. As of this writing, she has not gotten her laptop, but I have no doubt if she keeps creating, it is on its way.

My daughter loves rocks. She has from a very early age. Yesterday we took our first trip to a rock shop, and it was love beyond all telling. The man at the shop showed us how he cuts stone and can cut crosses and other shapes out of the stone. My daughter was fascinated. As we left, we talked about her getting a stone cutting saw so she can make her own creations out of stone.

She has recently gotten into creating things out of wood, and I know the two fit together. Learning one will advance her capacity to learn the other. In her eyes, I see the God of creation. Maybe that's why I like to write. I love the feeling of creating meaning by the patterned arrangement of 26 letters and 10 numbers. The greatest works of the world like the Bible were created using just these 36 characters. Think about that for a moment. It's astonishing, is it not?

What makes them masterpieces is the sheer ability to create, and someone else can create something equally amazing with the same 36 characters. You don't have to compete to use them. They are yours, and they are limitless.

The more I concentrate on creating, the happier I become. There was a time in my writing career when I would read of the achievements of others and become annoyed. Why did they get the book contract and I didn't? I see now how entrenched in the worldly philosophy of competition I was. In this philosophy when someone else wins, I lose because if the contracts are limited, them getting a contract means there are fewer for me.

And the tragedy of this mentality goes way beyond this example.

I was talking with a friend of mine the other day about our girls' night out getting together night coming up. She said, "Okay, but this time I am paying because I need to pay you guys back." (She's new to our little group, so I understood where she was coming from.) I told her that among Holy Spirit friends paying is relative. We aren't keeping score—at all. I couldn't tell you who's ahead, who's not, who owes whom what, and it literally doesn't matter.

When I first started this little group, I intuitively "knew" it would be different than the way I had always done things. It started with another friend of mine. I began giving her gifts—books and other uplifting things. After about the fifth thing that I'd brought over for no reason other than I wanted to (it wasn't her birthday or even a special day on the calendar), she protested, "Staci!" To which, I said, "No. It's not about you having to pay me back. It's only about... I want to share with you what I have. I want to share the blessings in my life."

As I told our new Holy Spirit friend, I have so many blessings flowing through my life, it is natural to me to share what I have with others. She said something that sounds very good, "Yea, but I just want to pay my fair share." Ah. That's the way the world thinks. "I must pay. I must pull my own weight. I must give my fair share, or you will not want to be around me."

In worldly terms this makes sense. If I pay for your meal and my resources are limited, then you'd better pay me back or I now have less because of you. In other words, you owe me to bring me back to even. But that's not how it works in a creation-based paradigm. From a creation-based perspective, I have what I need because if the resource is not here, it can be created or obtained through my creation of something else in order to trade for the resource. Think of the resources now using a different term—blessings. The unlimited blessings in my life flow through me onto you when I pay for your meal. That doesn't mean I now have less because I gave you some. In fact, and you know this in relation to love, the more love I give away the more I have.

That's how it is with God. The more you give away, the more you have. In a creation-based reality, the resources are not limited—they are limitless. If you need more, you simply ask for more or better yet create more. More and more and more is available if you focus on God's resources and learn to create just as God does. As you do this, you will let go of fear-filled, limited, competition thinking and being, and more will be added to you.

"Seek ye first the kingdom of God (create and creation), and all these things shall be added unto you." Learn to create. Let go of having to compete. It will change everything. (2005)

Recommended Resources

Peterson, Eugene, *The Message Bible Remix: The Bible in Contemporary Language*, (Navpress, 2003).

Walt Disney Pictures, *The Chronicles of Narnia: The Lion, The Witch, and The Wardrobe,* (Walt Disney Pictures, 2005).

Father Robert E. Barron, *Untold Blessings: Three Paths to Holiness*, (wordonfire.org, 2005).

Friday Night Lights LLC, *Friday Night Lights,* (Friday Night Lights LLC 2004).

Brennan Manning, *The Ragamuffin Gospel*, (Multnomah Publishers, 2000).

LucasFilms, *Star Wars III: Revenge of the Sith,* (20th Century Fox, 2005).

Max Lucado, *Traveling Light*, (W Publishing Group, 2001).

John Ortberg, *If You Want to Walk on Water, You've Got to Get Out of the Boat, (*Inspirio/Zondervan, 2004).

Nancy Stafford, *Beauty by the Book: Seeing Yourself as God Sees You,* (Multnomah Publishers, 2002).

Bruce Wilkinson, *The Prayer of Jabez*: *Breaking Through to the Blessed Life,* (Multnomah Publishers, 2000).

Ludwig van Beethoven, *Ode to Joy.* Words by Friedrich Schiller.

Og Mandino, *The Greatest Miracle in the World,* (Bantam, 1983).

Jeff VanVonderen, *Families Where Grace is in Place,* (Bethany House, 1992).

Viktor E. Frankl, *Man's Search for Meaning*, (Simon & Schuster, 1984).

Andy Andrews, *The Seven Decisions*, (AcornMedia, 2005).

Keith Urban, "Days Go By," *Be Here*, (Capitol Records, 2004).

Neale Donald Walsh, *Communion with God*, (Berkley Trade, 2002).

Wallace D. Wattles and Ruth L. Miller, *The Science of Getting Rich*, (Atria Books/Beyond Words, 2007).

Mark Hall, Casting Crowns, *Live from Atlanta*, (Reunion, 2004).

About the Author

A stay-at-home mom with a husband, three kids and a writing addiction on the side, Staci Stallings has five previous Inspirational Romance novels *The Long Way Home*, *Eternity*, *Cowboy*, *Lucky*, *Dreams by Starlight*, and one collection of short stories, *Reflections on Life* in print.

Stallings has also been a featured writer in the *From the Heart* series, in *Chicken Soup to Inspire the Body and Soul*, *Soul Matters*, *God's Way for Mothers* and in numerous inspirational, spiritual, and family-oriented ezines across the Internet. Although she lives in Amarillo, Texas, and her main career right now is her family, Staci touches many lives across the globe every week with her blog, "Homeward Bound" at http://stacistallings.blogspot.com/.

Read articles, e-books, and previews of Staci's books at:

http://www.stacistallings.com

You'll feel better for the experience!

Also Available from Staci Stallings

THE LONG WAY HOME

City-bred Jaxton Anderson thinks he knows more than the "country hicks" in Kansas ever will. However, one intriguing farm girl, Ami Martin, who is about as welcoming as the thorns on the rosebushes in her garden, and a grandfather Jaxton hasn't seen in years soon convince him that he doesn't have as much figured out as he thought. The harder Jaxton tries, the worse he makes things until a series of crises force him to reevaluate himself and the ideals he has always held to be important in this life.

Winner of the WordWeaving Award for Excellence

ETERNITY

Aaron Foster is in a bind. His fiancée has dumped him and moved out. Then to Aaron's horror, his new roommate, Drew Easton, unwittingly comes home with her. To save Drew's heart, Aaron conspires with his best friend, Harmony Jordan to break up Drew and Mandy by setting him up with Harmony. Unfortunately for Aaron, the plan works better than he could ever have imagined. Now with the tables turned, Aaron struggles with regret while remaining hopeful that somehow Harmony will come to want him as much as he now realizes he wants her.

REFLECTIONS ON LIFE

Fifty-two stories to encourage you on your journey. This book will compel you to look at each challenge in life as an opportunity to observe a miracle. It will encourage you to allow God to transform your ordinary life into an extraordinary one. It will remind you to reflect on your own life experiences and learn from them.

COWBOY

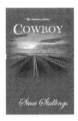

Cowboy is a grace-filled story about the power of giving everything to God and how a simple act of compassion can change lives forever. Emotional, soothing, and heart-wrenching, Cowboy is infused with the message that no matter who we are and no matter what life has thrown at us, we never have to walk alone.

LUCKY

Does a dream ever seem very far away because of stupid choices you've made? It does for Kalin Lane and Danae Scott. Kalin knows what he wants. Being patient as God works out the details is the issue. Danae is trapped in dreams others have for her. Both are struggling in lives they despise... until one night that changes everything.

DREAMS BY STARLIGHT

If all the world's a stage and each of us plays a part, then Camille Wright is the high school wallflower nobody remembers and only the bullies ever knew was there. But sometimes where you want to be isn't where you are destined to be at all...

Read the first three chapters of any Staci Stallings book at:

www.stacistallings.com/Previews.htm

You'll feel better for the experience!

Printed in Great Britain
by Amazon

59977249R00134